A GUIDE TO PORTRAIT STATUES IN CHICAGO'S LINCOLN PARK

Krista August

Lincoln Park Press
Chicago, Illinois

A Lincoln Park local, Krista August holds an undergraduate degree in mathematics from Northwestern University and a graduate degree in education from DePaul University.

Krista's art studies include classes at the Palette and Chisel, the Old Town Triangle Association, the School of the Art Institute of Chicago, Richeson School of Art, and the Peninsula School of Art.

For three years, she took great pleasure in researching, composing, and illustrating *Giants in the Park*.

Krista works part-time for an art gallery/frame shop, Art de Triumph and Artful Framer Studios, and for a math tutoring center, Mathnasium West DePaul. As a docent for the Chicago Architecture Foundation, she gives walking tours of Chicago's historic and modern skyscrapers.

Library of Congress Control Number: 2010918384

EDITOR: Laurel Haines
COVER AND INTERIOR DESIGN: Barbara Barg Medley
ILLUSTRATIONS: Krista August

On the cover: Statue of William Shakespeare

ISBN: 978-0-615-42737-9

Printed in the United States of America

To Ann — Enjoy the tour!. Krista

Contents

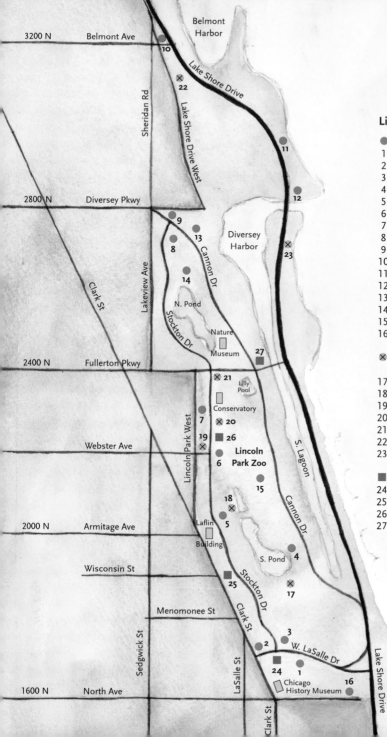

3200 N — Belmont Ave

Belmont Harbor

10

22

Lake Shore Drive

Lake Shore Drive West

Sheridan Rd

11

12

2800 N — Diversey Pkwy

9

13

8

Diversey Harbor

Cannon Dr

Lakeview Ave

14

Clark St

23

N. Pond

Stockton Dr

Nature Museum

27

2400 N — Fullerton Pkwy

21

Lilly Pool

Conservatory

7

20

Lincoln Park West

19

26

Webster Ave

6

Lincoln Park Zoo

15

18

5

2000 N — Armitage Ave

Laflin Building

S. Lagoon

Cannon Dr

S. Pond

4

Wisconsin St

25

Stockton Dr

17

Menomonee St

Clark St

Sedgwick St

2

3

W. LaSalle Dr

24

1

LaSalle St

Chicago History Museum

16

1600 N — North Ave

Clark St

Lake Shore Drive

N

Lincoln Park Monuments

● **PORTRAIT STATUES**
1 Lincoln
2 La Salle
3 Franklin
4 Grant
5 Andersen
6 Schiller
7 Shakespeare
8 Hamilton
9 Goethe
10 Sheridan
11 The Alarm
12 Signal of Peace
13 Altgeld
14 Oglesby
15 Field
16 Black

✕ **MISSING PORTRAIT STATUES**
17 Garibaldi
18 Andersen
19 Beethoven
20 Solti
21 Linné
22 American Doughboy
23 Swedenborg

■ **OTHER MONUMENTS**
24 Couch Tomb
25 Kennison Boulder
26 Bates Fountain
27 Curve XXII (I Will)

Preface

Located two-plus miles north of Chicago's downtown, Lincoln Park names both a neighborhood and a park—Chicago's largest park, boasting some six miles of lakefront.

This big-city playground proudly hosts sixteen vintage portrait statues. The reader can read all about them—the heroes and the monuments—amid the watercolor-rendered illustrations of this guidebook. For curious locals and interested tourists, this self-guided walking-tour publication combines biography, Chicago history, and sculpture content. Seven missing statues are detailed as well.

As for the route, this sculpture tour zigzags north and loops back south to exceed a distance of four miles, so it is perhaps best accomplished over several outings—or on a bike!

Art trekkers may note that marked monuments on the *Giants in the Park* map are keyed to correspond to numbered chapters.

And so I invite you to Lincoln Park, the park, to see Chicago through the prism of our forefathers' heroes.

Krista August
www.lincolnparkstatues.com

Acknowledgments

Thanks very much to employees of the Chicago Park District who assisted me with this project, specifically Julia Bachrach, park district historian, and Michael Fus, preservation architect. Some information is not available in print form, and in these instances, their expertise, access to documents, and willingness to help was invaluable. Thanks also to Susan Fargo, vice president of the Lincoln Park Conservancy, for the time she took on some fact checking.

Particularly helpful were the librarians at the Municipal Reference Collection desk and the Visual and Performing Arts Information Center at the Harold Washington Library.

While I never contacted Pamela Bannos, I did attend her lecture at the Chicago Architecture Foundation, and her website, www.hiddentruths.northwestern.edu, was a major source for me as I composed my introduction.

I am grateful to my editor, Laurel Haines, for judiciously helping me set the book's final text. And to editors in the earlier stages of the manuscript—Kristi Turnbaugh, Caroline Lahrmann, and Lara Brown—I benefited from your many good comments.

Securing author and wordsmith Cynthia Clampitt as my proofreader was a windfall. Polish and precision follow in her path.

Likewise, I was enormously fortunate in working with Barbara Barg Medley, who was a wizard with the book's cover and interior design, as well as the patient and professional David Bullard of Lazare Printing.

My family, Mom, Dad, Lance, Jon, Caroline, and their families, provided the necessary support and feedback to complete this adventure. They were in many ways my partners in writing *Giants in the Park*.

To many unnamed friends, who listened to and advised me on my project, I will always be thankful.

Lastly, I must single out Sebastian, who, though in Argentina, offered encouragement and long-distance input. He read every word and critiqued every illustration throughout the book's entire undertaking. I could not have completed this guidebook without his confidence.

Introduction

Lincoln Park: A Complicated History

A CEMETERY

Near the southeast corner of Clark Street and West LaSalle Drive rests a mysterious marker, Couch Tomb, final resting place of at least one early Chicagoan. Once purposefully shrouded by landscaping, this recently restored mausoleum quietly hints that Lincoln Park has a hidden past.

A few blocks north of Couch Tomb, just east of where Wisconsin Street meets Clark Street, a boulder approximates the burial site for another early Chicagoan, David Kennison.*

Often overlooked, these artifacts are reminders of a time when Lincoln Park was, in fact, Chicago City Cemetery.

For more than twenty years, 1843 to 1866, Chicago's deceased were buried near North Avenue and the shoreline. By 1846, these grounds included family lots, a Catholic cemetery, a Jewish cemetery, and a potter's field, traditionally a place for the unknown and the indigent.† During active burial years, an estimated thirty-five thousand people were laid to rest in Chicago's marshy lakefront.[1] Tombstones, wooden or stone, as well as mausoleums and sculptures, marked gravesites of the rich and poor.

By the early 1850s, the city's growth had made the cemetery's location a nuisance, and citizens began to petition its removal. Nevertheless, City Cemetery expanded north to just beyond Wisconsin Street, as burial plots in the old cemetery filled up.

In 1859, Dr. John H. Rauch of Rush Medical College alarmed citizens when he claimed that dead bodies along the shoreline contaminated city drinking water, causing sickness. After enduring deadly cholera outbreaks for much of the prior decade, Chicago's citizenry was highly fearful. The city quickly reacted

---

* At the time of his death in 1852, Chicagoans believed David Kennison to be 115 years old, the last survivor of the Boston Tea Party, and a Revolutionary War soldier. Historians have disputed these claims.

† Originally Chicago City Cemetery lay between North Avenue and Menomonee Street, east of Clark Street. The Catholic Cemetery was located south of North Avenue, further bound by Schiller Street, Dearborn Street, and the lake (approximately today's Astor Street).

by halting the sale of burial plots in May 1859, although burials continued in the previously sold plots and in the potter's field until March 1866.[*]

By the mid-1850s, citizens began to plead for a public park using vacant cemetery land, approximately sixty acres located north of Wisconsin Street and south of present-day Webster Avenue. Pleas were answered in 1861, when city officials converted unused cemetery acreage to parkland, known as Cemetery Park by 1863. The more alluring name of "Lake Park" was formally adopted in October 1864, only to be changed eight months later to "Lincoln Park." While the City of Chicago was clearly honoring recently assassinated President Lincoln, the name-change resolution cited an alternative reason: "Whereas, . . . there are now two public parks designated by the name 'Lake Park' therefore Resolved, . . . the unoccupied portion of the old Cemetery grounds Shall be hereafter known and designated as Lincoln Park."[2, †]

Quickly the city set to beautifying the new park's natural landscape. In September 1865, landscape designer Swain Nelson was hired, and by November 1865, park transformation commenced. Nature had left Lincoln Park an uneven vista of sand dunes and swamps, formed by an ever-evolving shoreline. Groves of scrub oaks and white ash accented the acreage. Under the direction of Nelson, sand dunes became fertile hills and swamps morphed into ponds or lawns. Trees, shrubs, and rocks were added as well as drives, walkways, bridges and fountains.

In 1868, New York's Central Park gifted two pairs of swans to Lincoln Park, the first animals in a later burgeoning population of creatures that would one day form Lincoln Park Zoo. Central Park's commissioners added that the donated swans were "of the stock presented several years since to our park by the cities of Hamburg and London, and will be with you, as they have been with us, a great popular attraction."[3]

A PARK MINUS A CEMETERY

In 1861, the body of nineteen-year-old Frances Pierce and her ten-month-old baby, who both died in 1854, were moved from Chicago City Cemetery to Rosehill

---

[*] It is estimated that nearly four thousand deceased Confederate soldiers from Chicago's notorious prisoner of war camp, Camp Douglas, were buried in the potter's field between 1862 and 1865. Many of these rebel remains were likely never removed. The potter's field was transformed into park baseball fields in 1877.

[†] The first "Lake Park" extended along the lake east of Michigan Avenue, south of Randolph Street, nearly to 12th Street.

Cemetery. Their sculptured tombstone, completed by artist Charles B. Ives in 1856, of mother with baby in repose, was monumental.

As early as 1859, families began to remove bodies from City Cemetery, after Chicago's first rural cemetery, Rosehill, opened in July of that year. Rural cemeteries were a natural development as Chicago's growth continued to accelerate. Over the next decade or so, until the Chicago Fire of 1871, a large number, but likely less than half, of City Cemetery bodies were removed and reinterred elsewhere.[4,*]

In 1869, The Lincoln Park Act made the cemetery and the park the responsibility of the Lincoln Park Commissioners.[†] With this act, commissioners gained the power to acquire cemetery land for park purposes, by condemnation and purchase. Six months following lot condemnation, park commissioners could rightfully and decently dispose of any unclaimed bodies. The Lincoln Park Act also annexed additional lakefront property, north of the park to Diversey Avenue.

A PARK MINUS A CEMETERY—AFTER THE FIRE

The modern stainless-steel column just north of Fullerton Parkway at Stockton Drive marks the approximate northernmost point that the Chicago Fire reached. This sculpture, by Ellsworth Kelly (1981) and nicknamed *I Will*, celebrates the can-do spirit that Chicagoans exhibited in rebuilding the city from ashes.[‡]

The Chicago Fire of October 8, 1871, ravaged the years-neglected cemetery. The hordes of people who fled the fire north trampled cemetery grounds. The fire's heat and flames consumed wooden and stone tombstones. As a result, many gravesite locations were lost, and consequently bodies interred within would never be exhumed. Northwestern University senior lecturer Pamela Bannos estimates on her website, hiddentruths.northwestern.edu, that, conservatively, more than ten thousand unclaimed bodies were left behind, as park commissioners transformed the cemetery into part of Lincoln Park.[§]

---

[*] In addition to Rosehill Cemetery, other cemeteries which reinterred bodies from City Cemetery included Graceland, Oak Woods, Catholic Cavalry, German Lutheran (Wunder's), and the Jewish Cemetery.

[†] Before the Lincoln Park Act of 1869, the cemetery and parklands were under the jurisdiction of the Board of Public Works.

[‡] Ellsworth Kelly's sculpture at Fullerton Avenue and Stockton Drive is titled *Curve XXII*. Its shape suggests the modern skyscrapers that Chicago "gave birth to" after the fire.

[§] After the fire until the late 1880s, exhumations continued from City Cemetery. In 1998, while constructing the History Museum's parking facility at North Avenue and West LaSalle Drive, partial remains of eighty-one individuals were unearthed.

One tombstone not destroyed by the fire, Couch Tomb, still stands near the Chicago History Museum. There is no precise explanation for why this mausoleum remains. Banos speculates "no one would assume the financial responsibility for removing it during the cemetery's transition into pleasure grounds."[5] Since the structure would survive the cemetery's demise, the city apparently resolved to minimize its visibility. On February 18, 1877, the *Chicago Tribune* reported, "the Commissioners have determined to let it [Couch Tomb] remain, and plant trees thickly around it."[6] In 1999, after more than a century of neglect, Couch Tomb was carefully restored with monies generously contributed by the Elizabeth Morse Charitable Trust. Today it is a stately monument honoring Lincoln Park's spirited past.[*]

THE PARK OF A WORLD-CLASS CITY

On October 11, 1893, the cornerstone was laid for the Chicago Academy of Sciences Building, also named the Matthew Laflin Memorial Building, located in Lincoln Park at the termination of present-day Armitage Avenue. This nature museum, founded in 1857, housed a natural science library and collection. At age ninety-two, Matthew Laflin, one of Chicago's early settlers, donated $75,000 toward construction of the $100,000 structure.[†]

Leading up to the World's Fair of 1893 and beyond, there was a developing desire among Chicago's civic leaders and millionaires to fashion Chicago into a world-class city, culturally rich in the arts and sciences, not just a money-getting pig town. In 1868, Chicago Historical Society cofounder, Isaac Arnold, made a speech to fellow society founders imploring Chicagoans to "encourage and honor men of culture, letters, and science." He said, "It is time . . . for a new advance. We have boasted long enough of our grain elevators, our railroads, our trade in wheat and lumber, our business palaces; let us now have libraries, galleries of art, scientific museums, noble architecture and public parks . . . and a local literature; otherwise there is danger that Chicago will become merely a place where ambitious young men will come to make money and achieve fortune, and then go elsewhere to enjoy it."[7]

---

[*] Couch Tomb was built for Ira Couch who died in 1857. Couch was a Chicago millionaire who accumulated wealth as an innkeeper and in real estate. He had owned the Tremont House, a hotel once located at Dearborn and Lake Streets. No one knows how many bodies are entombed inside.

[†] Today the Chicago Academy of Sciences is the Peggy Notebaert Nature Museum in Lincoln Park at Cannon Drive and Fullerton, and the historic Laflin Memorial Building houses Lincoln Park Zoo offices. Matthew Laflin created wealth by selling explosives for the building of the Illinois Michigan Canal.

Chicago's elite demonstrated their acceptance of the responsibility of their privilege and power with the establishment and funding of important cultural institutions: the Art Institute of Chicago, established, 1879; the Newberry Library, conceived in 1868 and established, 1887;* the Auditorium Building, completed in 1889; the University of Chicago, founded, 1890; the Chicago Symphony Orchestra, organized, 1890; Armour Institute (Illinois Institute of Technology) opened in 1893; The Field Museum, incorporated, 1893; the Chicago Academy of Sciences Building, completed in 1894; and Yerkes Observatory, instituted in 1897.

In April 1890, ambitious Chicago won its bid to host the World's Columbian Exposition, held 1893. With architecture and sculpture being a focal point, Chicago attracted many talented artists and sculptors to the city in the years leading up to the fair.

At a time when cities were dark, dangerous, and dirty, the fair exhibited a pristine vision of what a city could be: clean, bright, orderly, and beautiful. And what did the millions of fairgoers see in addition to stunning architecture? They saw monumental and enchanting sculpture. The fair's utopian White City featured 295 pieces of statuary, mostly temporary forms.[8]

It was against the backdrop of this environment that Chicagoans began to commission statues for their parks.

Lincoln Park monuments contributed by prominent individuals include: The Alarm (1884), Abraham Lincoln (1887), Rene-Robert Cavalier de La Salle (1889), Signal of Peace (1894), William Shakespeare (1894), Benjamin Franklin (1896), Ludwig von Beethoven (1897), and Alexander Hamilton (gifted 1928, unveiled 1952).

Chicago's strongly bonded ethnic groups were an equally inspired force contributing bronzes representing heroes of their fatherlands. Lincoln Park received gifts of sculpture from the Swedes, Germans, Danes, Italians, and Norwegians. Honored figures included Carl von Linné (1891), Friedrich von Schiller (1894), Hans Christian Andersen (1896), Giuseppe Garibaldi (1901), Johann Wolfgang von Goethe (1914), Emanuel Swedenborg (1924), and Captain Magnus Andersen (1936).

---

* Upon his death in 1868, Walter Loomis Newberry called for a "FREE PUBLIC LIBRARY" with his gift of two million dollars. By the time of realizing his intentions, however, the Chicago Public Library had already opened in 1873. Consequently, Newberry trustees established a research library.

The general public and elected representatives participated by commemorating national and local heroes: Ulysses S. Grant (1891), John P. Altgeld (1915), Greene Vardiman Black (1918), Richard J. Oglesby (1919), Eugene Field (1922), Philip Henry Sheridan (1924), and The Spirit of the American Doughboy (1927). Portrait monument donations came to a near halt with the onset of the Great Depression in the 1930s and World War II in the 1940s, after which time, public art became increasingly abstract and more commonly created for city spaces, corporate offices, and sculpture parks.

Altogether, by 1952, Chicago's North Side park had acquired twenty-two portrait statues, sixteen of which remain today.* Since then, the George Solti bust was accepted in 1987, but later relocated in 2006. And far north in the park, just beyond Wilson Avenue, the Dr. Jose Rizal monument was installed in 1999.

LINCOLN PARK TODAY

In the summer of 2009, Lincoln Park Zoo began its restoration of South Pond, to create a more hospitable and inviting environment for wildlife and people. After dredging, deepening, and incorporating a natural landscape with soft edges—no more concrete-and-steel perimeter—animal and plant life should thrive.

Lincoln Park beautification and improvement efforts have continued for a century and a half. A series of landfill projects between the 1880s and the 1950s expanded the park to its current size: 1,208 acres.† Park advocates continually work to maintain and upgrade the park's natural setting and amenities: its beaches, harbors, ponds, lily pool, conservatory, zoo, museums, theater, rowing canal, sports facilities, restaurants, structures, and its historic statues.

Although vandals have targeted the park's monuments—most unfortunately by stealing the Beethoven and Emanuel Swedenborg busts in 1971 and 1976 respectively—Lincoln Park's historic art has more notably been the object of care.

In June 1987, the Friends of Lincoln Park, newly renamed the Lincoln Park Conservancy, organized an Adopt-a-Monument Program to refurbish

---

* The six statues that have since been removed are The Spirit of the American Doughboy, Beethoven, Swedenborg, Linné, Garibaldi, and Magnus Andersen.

† The 1930s saw an organizational change in the park's operation when Lincoln Park Commissioners became part of the Chicago Park District.

the park's vintage statuary as vandals, acid rain, and environmental pollutants have threatened their longevity. Adopt-A-Monument co-chairs, Margot Pritzker and art historian Mary Gray, spearheaded the effort and invited private sector participation. While the program is no longer active, three monuments were successfully restored: the Lincoln statue, funded in 1989 by the Sara Lee Corporation, and adjacent garden landscaping paid for in 1989 by Credit Agricole; the Shakespeare statue, endowed in 1989 by the Edelstein and Pritzker Foundations; and the Bates Fountain, financed in 1999, in part by Borg Warner Corporation.

In the absence of private sector contributions, the Chicago Park District oversees the ongoing responsibility of monument maintenance. In the first decade of the 2000s, at least six statues have undergone maintenance, repair, and/or restoration: La Salle (2000), Goethe (2001), Shakespeare (2003), Signal of Peace (2005), Lincoln (2008), and Andersen (2009). Park district preservation architects plan for and schedule future work as needed, and as funding is made available.

Lincoln Park remains an ever-evolving affair, an enchanting mixture of old and new. The park's monumental art invites us to explore the old: to study the heroes of our Chicago forefathers; and through examining the realization of their likenesses, to glimpse moments and ideals from our great city's youth.

Alike are life and death,

When life in death survives,

And the uninterrupted breath

Inspires a thousand lives.

Were a star quenched on high,

For ages would its light,

Still travelling downward from the sky,

Shine on our mortal sight.

So when a great man dies,

For years beyond our ken,

The light he leaves behind him lies

Upon the paths of men.

(Henry Wadsworth Longfellow, excerpt from "Charles Sumner")

KAUGUST

1

Abraham Lincoln

SIXTEENTH PRESIDENT OF THE UNITED STATES

1809–1865

I claim not to have controlled events, but confess plainly that events have controlled me. Now, at the end of three years struggle the nation's condition is not what either party, or any man devised, or expected. God alone can claim it.[9]

Abraham Lincoln, April 4, 1864[*]

ithout a single electoral vote from ten Southern states, Abraham Lincoln won the 1860 presidential election. Before he was sworn into office, seven Southern states seceded from the Union. And so, Lincoln's entire time in office was spent as the leader of a nation warring with itself.[†]

It was the Lincoln-Douglas debates from the 1858 Illinois U.S. Senate race that first earned Lincoln national recognition and the chance to run for President. The Lincoln-Douglas debates focused on the topic of slavery. As the senatorial candidate of the newly formed Illinois Republican Party, Lincoln promoted the core principle of his party's platform: opposition to the extension of slavery. In the debates, Lincoln defined the campaign's central controversy as "the difference between the men who think slavery a wrong and those who do not think it wrong."[10, ‡]

At the outset of the Civil War, Lincoln was careful to frame the contest as simply one of union versus disunion. Abolishment of slavery was not yet a popular enough cause on which to wage war. By the end of the war, in large part due to Lincoln's masterful handling of policy and public sentiment, Lincoln was able to broaden the aim of the war to also include human equality. The President's carefully crafted Gettysburg Address, in November 1863, extended the idea of human equality with the notion that this nation "conceived in Liberty . . . under God, shall have a new birth of freedom."[11]

---

[*] Abraham Lincoln was not a religious man until he became president of a nation at war.

[†] The American Civil War, April 12, 1861, to April 9, 1865, was the costliest war in American history in terms of American lives lost.

[‡] Lincoln lost this, his second, bid for the U.S. Senate seat.

It is remarkable that a man with less than one year of formal education led the nation through the Civil War.* Abraham Lincoln alone formulated war policy. He alone crafted the language of his policies, policy defenses, and speeches. Nearly every cabinet member complained of infrequent meetings and inadequate consultations. Lincoln's controversial war policies, which helped the Union achieve victory, included the suspension of the writ of habeas corpus, the Emancipation Proclamation, and the recruitment of blacks into the Union armies.†

Lincoln's skillful politicking in conjunction with some well-timed Union victories, most importantly General Sherman's taking of Atlanta, resulted in Lincoln winning a second term in the 1864 presidential race. In his second inaugural address, Lincoln shared with the American people his view of why the war was so prolonged.

He set up his explanation of the war's "magnitude or the duration" by first acknowledging that slavery was "somehow, the cause of the war," and by next quoting from Matthew: "Woe unto the world because of offences! for it must needs be that offences come; but woe to that man by whom the offence cometh!" Lincoln then concluded that God "now wills to remove" this offense and "gives to both North and South, this terrible war, as the woe due to those by whom the offence came." Lincoln viewed the North as sharing blame for helping to introduce slavery, for participating in the slave trade, and for protecting it under the Constitution. Lastly, Lincoln harshly concluded that if it is God's will, the war will continue "until all the wealth piled by the bond-man's two hundred and fifty years of unrequited toil shall be sunk, and until every drop of blood drawn with the lash, shall be paid by another drawn with the sword."[12]

As the war neared its close and then finally did close, Lincoln's last challenge was to formulate and manage reconstruction policy. On April 11, 1865, just two days after the South's surrender, Lincoln spoke to celebrating crowds outside the White House. His address touched on reconstruction policy, and he introduced the idea of suffrage for blacks.

In the crowd that night was a young actor and Lincoln hater, John Wilkes Booth, who for a time had been considering kidnapping and, most recently,

---

* Lincoln wrote on the subject of his education in the third person, "the aggregate of all his schooling did not amount to one year." Donald, *Lincoln*, 29.

† The suspension of the writ of habeas corpus gave the government authority to arrest and indefinitely detain, without a hearing or indictment, all persons thought to be aiding the Confederacy or seeking to overthrow the government. Although the Emancipation Proclamation did not immediately free many slaves, it was a major step toward ultimately abolishing slavery.

assassinating the president. Lincoln's idea of suffrage for blacks further enraged the twenty-six-year-old, and quickly Booth set to finalizing plans to salvage the Southern cause.

John Wilkes Booth shot Abraham Lincoln in the back, left side of the head on the night of April 14, 1865, while the President viewed *Our American Cousin* at the Ford Theatre. Lincoln never regained consciousness and died nine hours later. Lincoln left behind his wife, Mary Todd Lincoln, and two surviving sons of four born.*

Earlier on the day of his assassination, Lincoln shared with cabinet members a recurring dream that he had had the previous night. In his dream, while on water, "he seemed to be in some singular, indescribable vessel, and . . . he was moving with great rapidity towards an indefinite shore." Lincoln recalled that in the past this dream always returned before a Union victory, and then he named some of these victories. Although General Grant corrected him that one of the battles named was not a victory, Lincoln nevertheless judged that his dream was an omen for good news.[13]

THE LINCOLN STATUE

ARTIST   Augustus Saint-Gaudens (1848–1907)

DATE   October 22, 1887

BENEFACTOR Eli Bates (1805–1881)

LOCATION   Southeast of Clark Street and W. LaSalle Drive intersection; just east of the Chicago History Museum

PARTICULARS Eleven-and-a-half-foot-high bronze; granite setting designed by architect Stanford White (1853–1906) of New York firm McKim, Meade, and White. Two bronze spheres, which symmetrically decorate the ascending steps to the monument, have inscribed excerpts from Lincoln's two most famous speeches: his Gettysburg Address and his second inaugural address.

---

* Lincoln's twelve-year-old son, Willie, died during Lincoln's White House years, probably of typhoid. Pollution of the White House water system likely brought on the illness. Lincoln's second son, Edward, died of tuberculosis in their Springfield, Illinois, home in February 1850, just shy of his fourth birthday.

Chicago's most famous portrait statue, Lincoln Park's Lincoln statue, was the gift of businessman Eli Bates. Details of Bates's life recounted at the Lincoln statue unveiling ceremony on October 22, 1887, revealed the benefactor to be a man of great character.

Eli Bates was born into a large family of little means in Springfield, Massachusetts. This son of a common laborer suffered from a disease that required him to undergo an amputation at age sixteen, which left him crippled. The courage that Bates exhibited during this trauma compelled a Unitarian clergyman to take him into his home and educate him, as a member of his own family.

By age forty-four, Bates had found his calling in the Chicago lumber business, after years of changing jobs. Previously he had worked as a teacher in Massachusetts, New York, and Wisconsin, and as a lighthouse keeper in Milwaukee. As a pioneer lumber merchant, Bates made his fortune, and upon his death in 1881, his estate was valued at nearly $300,000. His friends estimated that during his life he quietly gave away an additional $100,000 to those in need.

Bates's will generously bequeathed monies to Chicago public causes: $25,000 to the Unity Church, $25,000 for the building of an industrial school as part of the Unity Church, $10,000 to the Chicago Athenaeum,[*] $5,000 to the North Star Dispensary for the sick and poor, $15,000 for a fountain in Lincoln Park, and $40,000 for a Lincoln statue in Lincoln Park.

The late Bates assigned the formidable task of erecting an Abraham Lincoln statue to his close associates James C. Brooks, Thomas F. Withrow, and George Payson. By the fall of 1882, after more than a year of devoted effort, these trustees had yet to name an artist. None of the American artists whom they had invited to submit models had created a winning design. And after paying for the first round of models and their transport, the trustees were in a bit of a quandary, having already exhausted funds set aside to pay for model submissions. The trustees, therefore, conceived an alternative approach, thereafter, to select a sculptor: they resolved to rely only on drawings and on an artist's proven ability, rather than on the traditional submission of models.

In seeking to secure for Chicago the finest Lincoln statue in existence, trustees Brooks and Withrow considered the Farragut statue in Madison Square that had so impressed them on their trip to New York City.[†] The Farragut statue

---

[*] The Chicago Athenaeum was an educational institution for young men of modest advantages. Courses in languages, literature, music, elocution, and drawing were offered for a nominal fee of ten dollars a year. Free lectures on popular topics and access to a gymnasium were additionally offered.

[†] David Farragut was a Civil War admiral for the Union.

by Augustus Saint-Gaudens had received resoundingly high praise both in the states and abroad, where it had been on exhibit in Paris in 1880. It was deemed to rank among the finest of American sculptures. Based upon this proven success and upon the artist's training, the trustees granted Mr. Saint-Gaudens the commission, with the freedom to create his own conception.*

Born of a French father and Irish mother, Augustus Saint-Gaudens was raised in the United States. At age nineteen, he entered the art academy Ecole des Beaux Arts in Paris, and thereafter, Saint-Gaudens for four years studied sculpture in Italy. At the time of receiving the Chicago Lincoln commission, Saint-Gaudens was in his mid-thirties.

Saint-Gaudens and posterity were fortunate in that the life mask of Lincoln's face and the cast of his hands were in existence. Leonard W. Volk of Chicago had created these forms, the face mask in Chicago six weeks before Lincoln's presidential nomination and the hand cast at Lincoln's home the first Sunday morning after his presidential nomination. Understanding the potential value of his work, Volk had traveled with it on four transatlantic trips, and so, auspiciously, they were in Rome at the time of Chicago's great fire. At one point, Volk made duplicates and gave the originals to his son, who had them stored at the New York Metropolitan Museum of Art. It was these stored original casts that Saint-Gaudens used for his creation.†

For three years, Saint-Gaudens devoted himself to a portrait commonly referred to as *Lincoln, the Man*. His profound labor was championed by the *Chicago Daily Tribune* days before the statue's unveiling:

> The entire aspect is so like the man, so devoid of artifice or paltriness, that, in spite of the homely features, it becomes majestic. It speaks at once
> . . . the troubled life,
> The conflict and the pain,
> The grief, the bitterness of strife,
> The honor without stain.[14, ‡]

---

* The trustees also awarded Augustus Saint-Gaudens the Lincoln Park fountain commission bequeathed by Eli Bates. The Bates Fountain is located near the west entrance of Lincoln Park Zoo. Other Chicago statues by Saint-Gaudens are the John Logan statue (Civil War hero) at Michigan Ave. and 9th Street (1897) and the Grant Park Lincoln statue (1926).

† Sculptor Leonard W. Volk was a leader of the Chicago arts movement, helping to found the Chicago Academy of Design (1867). Volk created the city's two oldest surviving monuments: the Volunteer Fire Fighters' Monument, erected in 1864, and Our Heroes, a monument to slain Union soldiers, installed in 1869. A third important Chicago work is his Stephen A. Douglas monument, completed in 1881.

‡ The *Chicago Daily Tribune* article quotes the second stanza of Henry Wadsworth Longfellow's poem "Charles Sumner."

Prominent sculptor Lorado Taft enthusiastically praised the monument's composition:

I remember what a surprise that empty chair gave us. It was so daring—so strange! One had only to imagine it eliminated, however, to realize promptly how essential it was in the composition. . . . It is one of the most ingenious devices of modern monumental art. All such considerations are forgotten, however, when one comes under the spell of the noble presentment.[15]

Lincoln's fourteen-year-old grandson, Abraham Lincoln, unveiled the Lincoln statue on a bitterly cold October day.* President Lincoln's sole surviving child, Robert Todd Lincoln, was present. When the flag dropped, a military band began to play "Hail Columbia," and a thirty-eight-gun salute commenced. The crowd of ten thousand erupted in cheers only momentarily, however, because the boom of the artillery spooked a horse attached to a buggy carrying two ladies. The frightened horse tore through the crowd and threw one of the women over its head when it tried to jump a fence. The fiasco ended with an entangled horse and two, fortunately, unhurt passengers.

The monument celebration concluded with a tribute to Lincoln by his old friend Leonard Swett. Mr. Swett's comprehensive outline of the occasion and the man closed with his personal and poignant memories:

The sublime and crowning characteristic of Mr. Lincoln, however, was his self-reliance. During the eleven years I was with him at the bar of this State I never knew him to ask the advice of a friend about anything. During the four years of his administration I never knew and never heard of his doing this. I never knew him in the preparation of a trial or the perplexity of it in court to turn to his associate and ask his advice. . . .

And yet he was the best listener I have ever known. He would hear any one on any subject and generally would say nothing in reply. He kept his own councils or his bottom thoughts well. He weighed thoroughly his own positions and the positions of his adversary. He put himself in his adversary's position or on the opposite side of a question, and argued the question from that standpoint. . . .

---

* Abraham Lincoln, the grandson, died in 1890 at sixteen of complications from minor surgery.

And here may I be permitted to mention another very remarkable and useful trait of his character. It was that mental equipoise which is disturbed at nothing. . . . He was a monument of strength upon which even the great men of the Nation, and men of his own Cabinet, could lean for strength. In moments of victory, when everybody else was carried away by the joyousness of the occasion, Mr. Lincoln had the same mental equipoise and was self-restrained and determined as before. In short, he was the strong man in the great contest, and the great men at Washington all learned to gain renewed courage from his calmness and to lean upon his own great arm for support.[16]

2

René-Robert Cavelier, Sieur de la Salle

FRENCH EXPLORER
1643–1687

Today, April 9, 1682, I . . . do take possession in the name of His Majesty and successors of his crown, of this country of Louisiana. . . . We are the first Europeans who have come down or gone up the said Colbert River [Mississippi River].[17]

René-Robert Cavelier, Sieur de la Salle

ené-Robert Cavelier, Sieur de la Salle was the first European to travel the full length of the Mississippi River. Upon reaching the river's mouth in 1682, La Salle claimed for France the Mississippi River and all the land it drained. This new territory was three times the size of France itself, and La Salle named it *Louisiana* in honor of his king, King Louis XIV.

La Salle's quest to explore the Mississippi began in 1668 when he first learned of this great river from American Indians. While living near Montreal, La Salle befriended Seneca Iroquois who spoke of a beautiful river that took eight or nine months to navigate. The Senecas claimed this beautiful river (which they called the Ohio) flowed into the sea.

For more than 150 years, European explorers had dreamed of discovering a northern route to reach the Orient. Trade with the Far East, through this legendary Northwest Passage, represented potential means to create enormous wealth. So when La Salle first contemplated a great river in the interior continent that led to a sea, he undoubtedly hoped that it drained into the Pacific Ocean.*

Over a thirteen-year period and under the harshest of conditions, La Salle doggedly pursued his goals of traveling the Mississippi to its end and extending the French domain.

First, La Salle sought the great river's source. Adventurer Louis Jolliet, whom La Salle encountered on his initial expedition in 1669, advised La Salle to

---

* Lucrative oriental commodities included spices, rare woods, precious stones, and silks.

go by way of the Upper Great Lakes. However, to La Salle, such a route seemed an unnecessary detour north. Instead, from the southern end of Lake Ontario, La Salle proceeded south. Hardships endured caused all to abandon him. Alone, La Salle reached what is today the Ohio River and descended it to near present-day Louisville before cautiously turning back.[*]

La Salle's next well-documented attempt to seek and probe the Mississippi would not commence until November 1678. (By this time, the river's end-point had been surmised from the 1673 campaign of Louis Jolliet and Jacques Marquette.[†]) La Salle's series of campaigns beginning in 1678 were beset with setbacks: Men chronically deserted and stole from him, three ships carrying necessary provisions were wrecked,[‡] and doubting creditors back in Quebec and Montreal seized his assets. From as far advanced as the Illinois River, these misfortunes caused La Salle three times to return to his starting point (where Lake Ontario flows into the St. Lawrence River); twice the return trips were made by foot. Father Membré, a missionary companion on three of La Salle's explorations, summarized La Salle's hardships this way: "Anyone else would have thrown up his hand and abandoned the enterprise; but, far from this, with a firmness and constancy, that never had its equal, I saw him [La Salle] more resolved than ever to continue his work and push forward his discovery."[18]

Finally, in February 1682, La Salle and his party, for the first time, entered the Mississippi River, and by April, they had paddled their canoes to its mouth.

La Salle's major achievement rested in large part on his talents of persuasion and diplomacy in dealing with the various Indian tribes. Unlike other explorers, La Salle sought peace with the Indians, and he earned their respect with his fair and amicable dealings.

---

[*] On all subsequent attempts, including a 1671 expedition in which he reached the Illinois River, La Salle would travel by way of the Upper Great Lakes to seek the Mississippi. From Montreal and the St. Lawrence River, La Salle's expeditions traveled by way of Lakes Ontario, Erie, Huron, and lastly Michigan. On La Salle's final, successful expedition (around January 1682), he took the Chicago River to reach the Mississippi via the Des Plaines and Illinois Rivers.

[†] Jolliet and Marquette traveled as far south as the Arkansas River where they turned back for safety reasons. By determining the Mississippi River's endpoint, they had accomplished their mission. A northwest passage was still imagined to exist from some point off of the Mississippi River.

[‡] On August 7, 1679, the first full-sized sailing vessel took to the waters of the Great Lakes. Built by La Salle and his men, they named the ship *Griffon* after the mythological creature. It was last seen by La Salle on September 18, 1679. Presumably it wrecked.

Ill-fatedly, La Salle's ambitions were not yet satisfied with this hard-won success, and he set for himself a daunting new purpose: colonization of the Louisiana territory.

On July 24, 1684, La Salle commenced what would become a disastrous undertaking: a voyage from France of four ships and 280 passengers, mostly men and women to populate a new French colony at the mouth of the Mississippi. Upon reaching the "Spanish Sea" (the Caribbean Sea), the doomed voyage met its first costly mishap: one vessel was captured by Spaniards.

The remaining ships sailed to seek the mouth of the Mississippi, based on La Salle's calculation of its location, but they lost their way. An erroneous calculation by La Salle of the site's latitude, coupled with the fleet's inexperience in navigating the Gulf waters, bred tragedy.

La Salle's venture ultimately concluded with two wrecked ships and the death of nearly all remaining voyagers.* (One ship, as originally planned, did return to France.) While La Salle tried to locate the Mississippi by foot after reaching land, he would never again find it.

La Salle died by murder. Two years after landing, with 180 voyagers,† on the coast of present-day Texas, La Salle led a party of seventeen on a campaign to Illinois and Montreal, to secure aid for his struggling settlement. All the hardships thus far endured had fostered in some members of this group intense hatred. A handful of vengeful conspirators plotted murder, and within a matter of days, these brutes had killed off four men, including La Salle. La Salle died from a shot to the head on March 19, 1687, somewhere in what is now east Texas.

---

* In 1995, the Texas Historical Commission located in Matagorda Bay one of La Salle's wrecked ships, the *Belle*. The ship was carefully excavated, and its remains and artifacts were preserved for some future, permanent museum exhibition.

† Of the 180 who landed in Texas, nearly all died by disease, malnutrition, accident, conspiracy, or Indian raids. Some fell victim to attacks by rattlesnakes, buffalo, and alligators. Evidence suggests that a few did survive by living with the Indians.

THE LA SALLE STATUE

ARTIST	Count Jacques de la Laing (1858–1917)
DATE	October 12, 1889
BENEFACTOR	Lambert Tree (1832–1910)*
LOCATION	Northeast corner of Clark Street and W. Lasalle Drive†
PARTICULARS	Nine-foot-high bronze, atop a pink granite pedestal

Today, the La Salle statue appears to survey the street bearing the great explorer's name, Lasalle Street, Chicago's major financial boulevard. The La Salle memorial, however, was originally designed to represent a moment of important discovery, when this Frenchman was the first European to gaze upon a newfound inland river.

At a cost not publicized, Judge Lambert Tree contributed the La Salle monument to Lincoln Park.‡ Tree explained, "There is no historical character in the annals of Illinois more worthy of remembrance than Robert de La Salle. Lincoln Park is a fitting place in which to place a memorial to him, and I trust that other artistic monuments of the early explorers of this region will follow."[19]

While serving as the U.S. minister to Belgium under President Cleveland, Tree commissioned Belgian artist Count Jacques de la Laing to create the La Salle sculpture. In order to faithfully represent the adventurer's likeness and dress, Laing relied upon authentic pictures and prints from the archives of the French marine department.

On a cold, windy, and rainy October afternoon, a crowd of fifteen hundred people gathered to witness the unveiling of the statue of Robert de La Salle. At the ceremony's commencement, a letter of presentation from benefactor Lambert Tree was read. Tree wrote enthusiastically about La Salle's accomplishments:

---

* After his election to the circuit bench of Cook County in 1870, Tree made a name for himself fighting corruption and bribery in the city council. Charges made by Tree resulted in the convictions of nearly two dozen aldermen.

† The Lasalle statue was relocated several times. Originally the memorial stood farther north along Clark Street, between Wisconsin Street and Armitage Avenue. Around the year 2000, it was moved to its current location, from less than half a block north.

‡ In 1894, Tree would contribute a second statue to Lincoln Park of a Sioux warrior on horseback, entitled "A Signal of Peace." Tree also built the Tree Studios (1894–1913), located in River North, to entice artists working at the 1893 World's Fair to remain in Chicago.

He unquestionably discovered the Ohio and Illinois rivers, and . . . it is beyond controversy that he was the first white man who ever descended the [Mississippi] river to its mouth. . . .

He was a man devoted to great designs, from the pursuit of which neither danger, fatigue, famine, disease, disappointment, nor treachery could divert him. It is impossible to trace the immense course of his journeys on this continent through winter blasts and southern suns without arriving at the conclusion that he was a hero of the highest type, to whose geographical discoveries American civilization owes a heavy debt. To those of us whose lot has been cast on the shores of the great lakes and in the valley of the Mississippi he is a historical figure of the deepest interest, for it may be truly said that he was the first white man who penetrated the western wilderness and sent back word to Europe of the vast empire here that awaited the touch of the hand of civilization to bring it into being.[20]

After the statue's unveiling, keynote speaker E.G. Mason summarized the story of La Salle's life and accomplishments. Mason concluded:

It is well that in the park which bears the name and is adorned by the statue of Lincoln there should also stand the statue of another great man, identified, as he was, with the west, who, like Lincoln, fell by the assassin's hand, and like him wears the martyr's crown of one who gave his life for a great idea.[21]

KAUGUST

3

Benjamin Franklin

PRINTER, SCIENTIST, MINISTER TO FRANCE
1706–1790

All Europe is for us. . . . Tyranny is so generally established in the rest
of the world that the prospect of an asylum in America for those who
love liberty gives general joy, and our cause is esteemed the cause of all
mankind. . . . We are fighting for the dignity and happiness of human
nature. Glorious it is for the Americans to be called by Providence to this
post of honor.[22]

Benjamin Franklin, 1777[*]

"He snatched lightening from the sky and the scepter from tyrants," wrote a
Benjamin Franklin contemporary.[23, †]

In his eighty-four-year-long life, Benjamin Franklin played many roles:
printer, writer, businessman, moralist, scientist, inventor, politician, and
diplomat. Remarkably, he was exceptional in all his endeavors. But Franklin's
most profound contribution to posterity would be the image he helped create
for America's emerging identity: a country of *middling people* (his expression for
middle-class people), who were frugal, hardworking, and honest.[24]

Franklin's success as a Philadelphian printer allowed him to retire com-
fortably at age forty-two. His most notable achievement as a printer was his
humorous and witty *Poor Richard's Almanac*. In the almanac's twenty-five-year
run, Franklin sold as many as 10,000 copies yearly; 1,300-plus editions later, it
is still in print today. In *Poor Richard's*, Franklin sought to entertain and mor-
ally sharpen his readers with his many reworked old sayings, the most famous
being "Early to bed and early to rise, makes a man healthy, wealthy and wise."[25]

---

[*] As diplomat to France, Franklin wrote these inspiring words in an effort to win the hearts, minds, and ultimately the
financial and military support of the French.

[†] French statesman Turgot (1727–1781) poetically described Franklin with these words.

Retirement from printing permitted Franklin time to indulge his passion for scientific inquiry and experiment. Throughout his life he performed research on a variety of scientific unknowns: weather patterns, the Gulf Stream, and the earth's magnetism. He designed bifocal glasses, a clean-burning stove, and the glass armonica, a musical instrument that was for a short time fashionable. But it was his work with electricity that made him the most famous living scientist of the age. After making a breakthrough discovery known as the conservation of charge law,* Franklin began an inquiry into the connection between electricity and lightning. With a kite and key, Franklin managed to survive while collecting a lightning charge in a Leyden jar.† After conducting further experiments on the collected charge, Franklin confirmed "the sameness of electrical matter with that of lightning."[26] Consequently, deadly lightning, once thought to be an expression of God's wrath, was understood to be a tamable natural phenomenon.

Franklin was a model citizen dedicated to community betterment, so naturally he found his way into politics and government work. As an ordinary citizen, he conceived America's first subscription library, Pennsylvania's first fire-fighting club, America's first nonsectarian college (today University of Pennsylvania), and a volunteer Pennsylvania militia to answer the threat of the French and Indians.

As public issues in Pennsylvania and the colonies became more at odds with the British government, Franklin's political role became more elevated. Twice before the Revolutionary War's outbreak, Franklin traveled to London to lobby on behalf of the citizens of Pennsylvania (and later on behalf of Massachusetts's citizens, as well), remaining five and then ten years in London. Franklin sought compromise and harmony with England as a dedicated loyalist to the crown during this extended period, 1757 to 1775. It was only after years of snubs, stalemates, and ultimately British aggression that Franklin decisively joined the cause for independence.

On his last day spent in London before his return trip to Philadelphia in March 1775, Franklin's eyes teared as he read reports of the brewing war.[27] After more than fifteen years abroad, Franklin finally understood that imperial reconciliation was not possible. Franklin's sophisticated insight into the two distinct cultures was at the heart of his conversion: this newly forming nation of proud,

---

* Franklin's conservation of charge law asserted "that the generation of a positive charge was accompanied by the generation of an equal negative charge." Isaacson, *Benjamin Franklin*, 135.

† Some historians find Franklin's kite and key experiment doubtful. In *Benjamin Franklin: An American Life*, Walter Isaacson concludes that it is "unreasonable . . . to believe that Franklin fabricated the . . . facts of his kite experiment." Isaacson, *Benjamin Franklin*, 142.

hardworking, middling people would not stand in subordination to an elitist, rigid, hierarchical society.

Once the war began, Franklin, firmly in the rebel camp, played a central role. He was the only founding father to sign all four founding documents: the Declaration of Independence, the alliance treaty with France, the peace treaty with England, and the Constitution. Beyond signing them, he was intimately involved in their conception and drafting. Franklin's deep faith in the average citizen along with his fierce aversion to elitism guided his many enlightened contributions.

Franklin's greatest triumph of the Revolutionary War period and its aftermath was his masterful diplomacy with France (1776–1785). By winning and maintaining French aid and goodwill, Franklin secured America's victory in its fight for independence without entangling the still-forming nation in any international commitments.

After living to see Washington's first year as president, Franklin died quietly in his Philadelphian home surrounded by family and loved ones, sixteen years after his dutiful wife Deborah had passed away. While Franklin had lived apart from Deborah for much of their common-law marriage (she did not join him on his missions to London), he intended to join her in the ever after when, shortly before his death, he planned for their simple tombstone to read, "Benjamin and Deborah Franklin."

THE FRANKLIN STATUE

ARTIST	Richard Henry Park (1832–1902)
DATE	June 6, 1896
BENEFACTOR	Joseph Medill (1823–1899)
LOCATION	Just northeast of Stockton Drive and W. LaSalle Drive intersection*
PARTICULARS	Nine-foot-high bronze, atop a massive granite base

Chicago's first Benjamin Franklin statue was designed by Danish sculptor Carl Rohl-Smith and adorned the main entrance to the Electricity Building at the Columbian Exposition of 1893. This twenty-one-foot-high monument depicted Franklin, with a kite and key, head tilted back searching the sky. The Electricity

* In 1970, due to a Lincoln Park Zoo expansion, the Franklin statue was moved from its original location near the zoo.

Building was a major attraction at the exposition. Attendees were astounded by the many new electrical inventions presented: electric kitchens, an early facsimile, a device for viewing motion pictures, even an electric chair for executions. And Franklin, the man who "found electricity a curiosity and left it a science" was appropriately celebrated high atop a pedestal at the building's southern entryway.[28, *]

In 1895, when *Chicago Tribune* editor Joseph Medill offered to fund a Franklin monument for Lincoln Park, there were those who called for a duplicate of the World's Fair's statue by Rohl-Smith. Medill, however, had already commissioned Richard Henry Park.

Park, a native of New York State, studied in Florence, Italy, and relocated to Chicago before 1893, attracted by all the art commissions for the fair. He remained in Chicago after the fair until his death nine years later. For the Columbian Exposition, Park created a solid silver statue of *Justice,* using as the model Ada Rehan, a well-known actress. Park's *Justice* figure was featured at the Montana mining exhibit.

In creating a faithful Franklin likeness, Park had the advantage of studying an original Franklin portrait, painted by French artist Duplessis while Franklin resided in Paris as a diplomat. As was Medill's vision, the statue's design represents Franklin presenting his theory of lightning to a group of fellow scientists.

The unveiling ceremony for Lincoln Park's Franklin statue was held on a sunny afternoon, June 6, 1896. The crowd was predominately associates of the printing trade and its allied trades, as Medill had presented the bronze through the Old-Time Printers' Association of Chicago, of which he was a member.

Medill's approach to the lectern early in the ceremony elicited a warm reaction. He spoke at length, to recurring applause, of the man he considered "one of the three or four greatest men our country has produced."[29]

Following a near-tumultuous reaction to Medill's speech, Rene Bache, great-great grandson of Benjamin Franklin (through his daughter Sarah), released the drape revealing the nine-foot-high bronze atop its granite pedestal. As the crowd erupted in cheers, thirteen young girls, symbolic of the thirteen original states, adorned the sculpture with bouquets. Celebrations continued as a vocal quartet and band performed "The Star Spangled Banner" and, after further ceremonial formalities, "We'll Rally Around the Flag."

For the day's principal speaker, Medill had appealed to a young Chicago lawyer, H.D. Estabrook. Early in his speech, Estabrook established his theme:

* Franklin biographer Carl Van Doren (1885–1950) wrote, "He found electricity a curiosity and left it a science."

He [Franklin] discovered many secrets of nature, which he revealed to the world freely and without reserve. But of all his discoveries there was one of signal and paramount importance, the one which made him what he was, the one which virtually concerns every human being for all time to come . . . and which I have selected as the theme for what further I may have to say—the discovery of how to make life happy.

Estabrook related that one of Franklin's well-known recrafted sayings was a major tenant of Franklin's life: "Be virtuous and you will be happy." Estabrook continued:

But if this statue should serve no other purpose than a mnemonic to remind Americans that to be virtuous is to be happy it might be an anachronism in this age of mechanical substitution: but it harks back to a truth which Americans must some time learn—if not from Christ, why, then, from Benjamin Franklin. For, I repeat it, Franklin was happy, and happy because he was virtuous. His discovery was simply how to be virtuous.

With care, humor, and scholarly insight, Estabrook then detailed how Franklin made virtue an art and science. After describing Franklin's ledger and accounting process of honing thirteen identified virtues, Estabrook summed up the earnestness of Franklin's efforts[*]:

He did not trust absolutely in his own strength and resolution to achieve his purpose. He believed in prayer. . . . Night and morning he addressed to the throne of grace an invocation so earnest and yet so simple, so short, and yet so comprehensive: "O, powerful Goodness! bountiful Father! merciful Guide! Increase in me that wisdom which discovers my truest interest. Strengthen my resolution to perform what that wisdom dictates. Accept my kind offices to thy other children as the only return in my power for thy continual favors to me."[30]

Following Estabrook's inspiring analysis, the ceremony soon came to a close. The crowd had the pleasure of one more quartet performance, the singing of "Illinois." And lastly, all present joined together in singing "America."

---

[*] The thirteen virtues that Franklin worked to perfect as a young man were temperance, silence, order, resolution, frugality, industry, humility, justice, moderation, cleanliness, sincerity, tranquility, and chastity.

KAUGUST

4

Ulysses S. Grant

AMERICAN GENERAL AND EIGHTEENTH PRESIDENT
1822–1885

One of my superstitions had always been when I started to go anywhere, or do anything, not to turn back or stop until the thing intended was accomplished.

Ulysses S. Grant, 1844[31, *]

*P*erhaps Ulysses S. Grant was the only man in the Union at the time who could win the Civil War.[†] Our nation's first four-star general possessed a special blend of military genius and battleground character.

After taking supreme command of the Union army in March 1864, Grant dramatically evolved its operation, implementing new tactics that the United States would successfully employ for generations. Grant's vision of warfare was Napoleonic in that he relied on ever-mobile troops that sought to annihilate the enemy in bloody, costly battles.[‡] Grant understood that killing the enemy was the only way to end the war. Prior to Grant's taking charge, Union commanders had largely utilized the antiquated fighting method of controlling strategic locations, a relatively conservative strategy that lengthened the war and threatened empowerment of the Southern cause.

Grant's winning strategy was not without setbacks and tragic losses. More often than not, implementations did not go as planned, as is the rule in war.[32] But Grant's confidence and instincts on the battlefield were not to be rattled. Grant possessed a rare talent to read a battle and to improvise, despite imperfect

---

[*] Grant's words above are from his retelling of a story from his courtship with wife Julia. Stationed in St. Louis near Julia's home, Grant rode on horseback to visit her after a heavy rain. On his ride to see her, he was for a time stopped by a swollen creek, at which point he apparently considered his above quoted superstition. His story goes on to tell that he kept moving forward, in and across the creek, and emerged soaking wet on the other side.

[†] The American Civil War, April 12, 1861, to April 9, 1865, was the costliest war in American history in terms of American casualties. Approximately 620,000 Union and Confederate soldiers died, more than the combined totals of World War I, World War II, and the Korean War.

[‡] Grant disliked being compared to Napoleon. He maintained that European and U.S. conditions were so different that such a comparison was nonsensical. The methodology that Grant implemented utilized coordinated columns of converging troops that would envelope and ultimately trap the enemy.

information. When a maneuver did not work, he tried a new one, ever on the move and ever on the offensive because he understood that a defensive strategy was a losing one.

In the Wilderness Battle in May 1864, Confederate fighters lured advancing Northern soldiers into major combat, but in a wooded terrain that was not winnable for either side. After two days of fighting, the Union had lost close to fifteen thousand men, versus the eight to nine thousand that the Confederacy had lost. Interviewed at this sobering time by a *New York Tribune* reporter, a determined Grant replied to questions in bold fashion, stating that "things are going swimmingly down here." Moments after the interview ended, Grant followed after the interviewer to add in confidence, "If you see the President, tell him from me that whatever happens, there will be no turning back."[33]

In the hours of crisis in the Wilderness Battle, some Army of the Potomac soldiers began to express concern, and with good reason. This army of Northern fighters, newly under the command of Grant, had already been repelled six times in similar campaigns by General Lee's Southern fighters. The Army of the Potomac had great respect for Lee's abilities, and when Grant at first seemed unmoved by or perhaps unaware of Lee's skillfulness, at least one soldier spoke to him in earnest. Grant shot back impatiently, "I am heartily tired of hearing about what *Lee* is going to do. Some of you always seem to think he is suddenly going to turn a double somersault and land in our rear and on both our flanks at the same time. Go back to your command and try to think what we are going to do ourselves, instead of what *Lee* is going to do!"[34]

War was what Ulysses S. Grant was good at, war and riding horses. For years, Grant was probably the best horseman in all of the army.[35] His love of horses began in southwestern Ohio, when at the age of five, he jumped on the back of a pony and just held on when it tried to shake him off. As a West Point cadet, Grant, the best rider in his class, performed an astounding feat at a graduation show. He rode into an arena filled with dignitaries, and then at great speed charged toward and jumped over a bar set at six feet three inches, the highest jump at that time ever performed at the academy. As a soldier in the Mexican War,* Grant volunteered to ride out of Monterrey, Mexico, where bloody battles were being fought, in order to secure additional troops and ammunition. Accounts are that he rode out of the city on the side of the horse out of the line of enemy fire, one leg under the horse, hands gripping the horse's mane. And

---

* The Mexican War, 1846 to 1848, was fought, in short, over Texas.

in his first Civil War battle in November 1861 at Belmont, after having his own horse shot out from under him, Grant, while riding another's mount in retreat, got the horse to sit down on its haunches, slide down a muddy bank, and then negotiate an unstable plank onto the deck of a boat.

It is well known that Grant had a weakness for liquor, and detractors sometimes exaggerated this shortcoming. While alcohol often got the best of America's hero, ultimately Grant was in control in that he drank only at down times, presumably to help relieve stress or boredom.[36] Grant's drinking problem caused him early in his career to join a temperance movement. Apparently the only cure for his excessive drinking was the companionship of his beloved wife, Julia.

The shy and quiet Grant was a devoted family man. When his family was away, he missed them terribly and wrote them often. Whenever possible during the Civil War, he sent for Julia and his children to join him when conditions were safe. Their happy marriage produced three sons and a daughter.

Following the war, Grant rode his tidal wave of popularity to the White House. Without his seeking the office, Republicans in 1868 nominated him unanimously, and without his campaigning, the country voted him into office, twice (1869–1877). Grant's two terms as President generally receive unfavorable reviews, essentially due to widespread corruption at the time. While Grant was considered honest and clean, many of those around him were not.

Grant's accomplishments as President defy his near bottom-of-the-list presidential ranking. His achievements include initiating the work of surveying a Panama-canal route; establishing an important international law precedent by winning a $15.5 million award from Great Britain as penalty for profiting from the American Civil War; settling for the first time America's border with Canada; signing the Fifteenth Amendment, thereby giving citizens of all races the right to vote; signing a law which in effect destroyed the country's original KKK organization; vetoing the Inflation Bill proposed by Congress, thereby thwarting further economic catastrophe from the Panic of 1873; formulating an Indian peace policy* in order to better secure the welfare of American Indians; and lastly resuming construction of the Washington Monument in DC after a twenty-five year halt.

Grant came to despise his office of the presidency and refused to run for a third term. Once released from his leadership burdens, Grant took his wife and

---

* While well-intentioned, Grant's Indian peace policy would ultimately fail.

traveled Europe, the Middle East, and Asia, and was warmly greeted by crowds and dignitaries everywhere he went.* After more than two years of traveling abroad, with Julia refusing to go onward to Australia, they returned home via San Francisco and Chicago.†

Grant's retirement was headed for financial catastrophe, so he planned to provide for his family by writing his memoirs. Grant had been an avid reader all his life, and so writing was something at which he was quite adept. Completing *Personal Memoirs,* however, proved to be a last battle, as he wrote against time while suffering from throat cancer. In this final task, Grant showed the same determination and courage that he had as a soldier. Against the odds, he kept his illness at bay long enough to finish what many consider a nineteenth-century American masterpiece.[37]

THE GRANT STATUE

ARTIST	Louis T. Rebisso, designer (1837–1899); M.H. Mosman, foundry man
DATE	October 7, 1891
BENEFACTOR	Citizens of Chicago
LOCATION	On a ridge overlooking Cannon Drive, approximately in line with Wisconsin Street
PARTICULARS	Bronze, eighteen feet three inches high; including the massive granite base, the form reaches a height of sixty feet eight inches

"It was the people's day. In every respect it was a popular celebration. The Nation, the State, the city were present in the persons of their representatives, but the people dominated the occasion."[38] This is how the *Chicago Daily Tribune* described the celebration for the General Grant statue that was held Wednesday, October 7, 1891.

---

* The sultan of Turkey, Abdul Hamid II, gave Grant two valuable Arabian stallions, which were put to stud in the United States, thus improving American breeds.

† The Grants sailed from Philadelphia on May 17, 1877, and arrived back in San Francisco in September 1879. Although rootless upon their return, they soon settled in New York City. Chicagoans honored the returning hero with an eighty-thousand-person parade. Generals Sherman and Sheridan were present, as was Mark Twain. Twain described Grant as an "iron man" after observing how unaffected he was by all the adulation.

The day's public festivities began at one o'clock, when a procession of some twenty thousand people formed downtown on Michigan Avenue near the Auditorium Building. The participants that gathered were from all walks of life and included militia, veterans, sons of veterans, city police, civic societies of all kinds, and invited guests. The parade's many groups included Army of the Tennessee veterans, U.S. troops, Illinois National Guardsmen, U.S. Colored Troops, Scottish pipers, Italian cavalry, color-bearers, color guards, and high school boys.

Starting at two o'clock, the procession marched north on Michigan Avenue with select military men and policemen on horseback, and with distinguished, invited guests in carriages. With the many uniforms, waving flags, and competing music bands, the parade was colorful and lively. Patriotic tunes such as "Rally 'Round the Flag" and "Annie Rooney" rallied the participants and spectators alike.

From Michigan Avenue, the line of the march continued across the Rush Street Bridge,* north on Rush Street, and eventually east to reach Lake Shore Drive and ultimately Lincoln Park. Along the way, streets were lined with crowds of cheering onlookers, and the entire procession took about one hour and twenty-five minutes to view.

Mrs. Julia Dent Grant, widow of General Grant, and her son Ulysses S. Grant, Jr., viewed the beginning of the parade from Potter Palmer's† mansion on Lake Shore Drive, and then toward its halfway point, they joined the procession in a carriage.

On Lake Michigan, a marine procession paralleled the parade, as military vessels, fire-tugs, and private boats of all sorts carried spectators to view the celebration from the nearby water.

The idea for a Grant commemoration began within hours of learning of Grant's death on April 23, 1885. Promptly, Chicagoans, led by Potter Palmer, began contributing funds for the creation of a statue to celebrate the great soldier's life. Over one hundred thousand patriots donated amounts from $0.50 to $5,000, such that ample funds were collected before General Grant was buried.

To select the statue, noted artists of equestrian sculpture in the United States and Europe were invited to compete for a first, second, and third prize,

---

* At this time there was no Michigan Avenue Bridge; Michigan Avenue ended on the south side of the river.

† Potter Palmer was a Chicago millionaire who made his fortune as a dry-goods merchant. After selling his store and retiring, he returned to business as a real estate investor, most notably developing the Palmer House Hotel.

$500, $300, and $200 respectively.* In the fall of 1886, the trustees for the Grant monument fund awarded first prize to Louis T. Rebisso, an artist of Italian parentage who lived in Cincinnati. Mr. Rebisso was at that time a professor of sculpture at Cincinnati University.† The winning design appears to capture the General surveying an active battleground.

While Louis T. Rebisso designed the statue, M.H. Mosman of Chicopee, Massachusetts, cast the statue in bronze in nine separate pieces. The Grant bronze was the largest ever cast in the United States at the time, and the difficulties met in its casting delayed the project by at least a year. In June 1891, the form's 10,500 pounds were shipped to Chicago at a cost of $78.75. In Chicago, Rebisso and Mossman oversaw its piecing together. Altogether, the Grant monument, including the pedestal, cost an estimated $75,000.

After assembling the Grant likeness, it was covered from public view for months awaiting its official unveiling ceremony. In the granite masonry below the statue, a time capsule was placed which included various local artifacts: portraits of Chicago mayors, a Board of Trade annual report, a Chicago Harbor annual report, a report for the Army of Tennessee's 1889 proceedings, a copy of the *Chicago Tribune* and other local papers, subscription books of subscribers to the Grant Monument fund, and the list goes on.

Shortly after four o'clock on that October day, the ceremony was called to order, but its call was audible to few amid the cheering crowd, the piping bands playing "Red, White and Blue," and the still arriving procession. Early in the ceremony, survivors of the Twenty-First Illinois Infantry were recognized; these forty-some veterans were the first soldiers under Grant's command at the onset of the Civil War. The crowd warmly received these brave men as they carried their worn, old battle flag up to the monument.

The president of the Lincoln Park Commissioners, William C. Goudy, accepted the memorial from the trustees of the Grant memorial association, stating in part, "It is fit that this monument in honor of the great soldier should be placed in a park bearing the name of the illustrious President who chose him with wonderful sagacity as the leader of the Union armies. It seems appropriate

---

* Fourteen models from the Grant monument competition were placed on exhibition at the Art Institute in August, 1886.

† At the time of winning the Grant statue commission, Mr. Rebisso was best known for his equestrian statue of General James McPherson that stands in McPherson Park, Washington DC, a perhaps fitting connection. General McPherson had been a Union general under Grant in the Civil War and was mortally shot at the start of the Atlanta campaign on July 22, 1864. Grant's reaction to the news of McPherson's death was one of the few times he publicly displayed overwhelming emotion.

that statues of Lincoln and Grant should stand together on the shore of Lake Michigan and in the metropolis of the State which gave them to the Republic in its struggle for life."[39],[*]

With the acceptance official, a Miss Mary Strong, daughter of the late General Strong, pulled the cord that released the two veiling flags, and the throng of some 250,000 roared. The water vessels then joined in the tribute. Government steamers fired a twenty-one-gun salute. All other vessels blew their whistles for approximately a minute, and the fire tugs, with great personality, showed their capacity to throw water.

Meanwhile, Mrs. Grant was escorted forward before the beckoning crowd, where she struggled to show a smile as she wept. She bowed in appreciation, and the old soldiers in the front rows bowed back with deference.

The keynote speaker, Judge Walter Q. Gresham, closed the ceremony with a tribute primarily to the character of Grant, stating that, "Greatness was never more unconscious of itself than it was in him." In describing Grant's generous conduct toward the Confederacy after victory was secured, Gresham explained, "He thought more of giving an impulse to the pursuits of peace and industry amongst a disorganized people, of aiding them in the maintenance of themselves, of bringing them back into social as well as political relations with the rest of the country, than upon his own part and lot in the accomplishment of these salutary ends." Finally, Gresham highlighted Grant's love of peace, asserting that, "Although educated at West Point he was not a professional soldier. Instead of liking war he abhorred it as the greatest of human calamities, and his temperament inclined to peace."[40]

Shortly thereafter, the ceremonies closed. Mrs. Grant was escorted back to the Potter Palmer mansion. Hordes of people began dispersing from Lincoln Park, and marine vessels began their journey back to harbor. Yet the seemingly endless grand procession was still joyfully marching into the park at North Avenue.

---

[*] At the time the Civil War broke out, Grant was living in Galena, Illinois.

5

Hans Christian Andersen

DANISH WRITER OF FAIRY TALES

1805–1875

A poor child was I, and no one knew me,
But in my heart burned the poet flame;
It drove me bravely on in the world's bustle,
Though I had It alone and God in heaven.

To Denmark's king they led my feet,
I felt merely that I stood before a father,
Who gave my heart courage, my thoughts wings. –
And to the father heart I safely bring my song;
I do not see the throne where I kneel,
But in your eye: fatherly love.

Hans Christian Andersen, 1832

The above verse dedicated to King Frederick VI of
Denmark was published in Andersen's book
of poetry, *The Twelve Months of the Year.*

While Hans Christian Andersen authored novels, poems, dramas, and travel books, it was his fairy tales that made him wildly popular the world over. Today, Denmark's favorite storyteller, writer of some 150 fairy tales, is one of the world's most widely translated authors.

Andersen's genius was part of a revolutionary mindset that viewed and depicted children in a new and different way. He was one of the first authors to give children a voice and point of view in literature. Rather than presenting children in a traditionally passive light, Andersen radically elevated the stature of children, allowing them to speak their minds and express their hearts. One of Andersen's most memorable characters is the little child in "The Emperor's New Clothes." In Andersen's story, as the Emperor parades down the street in his underwear, only a child has the courage to declare, "But he isn't wearing anything at all!"[41]

Andersen's first fairy tales were mostly unique retellings of folktales that he had heard as a child or reinterpretations of tales from other countries. For example, "The Emperor's New Clothes" was Andersen's adaptation of an old Spanish fairy tale. Over time, though, he began to write more original stories inspired by his active imagination, his childhood memories, his own inner struggles, and his extensive travels.[*] "The Little Mermaid" and "The Ugly Duckling" are among his best-loved of these original tales.

Readers of Hans Christian Andersen's tales may be surprised by some of the tough, even horrifying, life realities that he depicted: orphaned children, dying children, evil stepmothers, death by broken heart, humans killing animals, mutilation, and decapitation. But Andersen's art is perhaps less surprising when it is understood to be, in large part, a reflection of the harsh and sometimes frightening realities of his own early years.[†] While he was fortunate to have had loving parents, life's painful situations were never far away. The women in his mother's family lived wretched lives: his grandmother, aunt, and half sister are all believed to have worked in a brothel at one time. His maternal grandmother was jailed for a week for mothering three children by different fathers.[‡] For a time, Andersen's paternal grandfather was locked up for madness. And, his own father was mentally ill in the final months of his life and died when Andersen was a child of eleven years. Because Andersen endured so much tragedy and despair in his early life, it is perhaps not difficult to understand how he learned to live life with his imagination on overdrive.

In addition to portraying life's cruelties in his stories, Andersen also wrote stories to express his own inner life. "The Little Mermaid," a story about a mermaid caught between the two worlds of land and sea, has been interpreted as a reflection of the author's conflicted sexual nature: Andersen's male side was apparently in conflict with a strong female drive. In "The Ugly Duckling," in which an ugly hatchling grows up to become a beautiful swan, Andersen

---

[*] Andersen's father encouraged him to travel, and he did. He took thirty extensive trips in his lifetime that amounted to nearly ten years on the road.

[†] A contemporary of Andersen, Søren Kierkegaard, asserted that the tension and tragedy in fairy tales actually help children to understand and resolve their own fears and anxieties.

[‡] Fyn, the Danish island where Andersen was born, was the region with the country's most illegitimate births. Prostitution was a means for survival for many lower class women.

depicts the path of his own life from an awkward, gangly and ostracized youth to an internationally famous author.

So how did Andersen escape the trap of his disadvantaged youth, where, in addition to family hardships, he endured sometimes humiliating social rejection for not fitting in with the other boys? At the tender age of fourteen, he left his home in Odense to make a life for himself in Copenhagen, the capital of Denmark. His heart was set on a life in theater, and so he devoted the next few years to succeeding in any way possible. After failing as an actor and ballet dancer, Andersen took up the challenge of writing for the theater as a last resort. While immediate success eluded Andersen in these early Copenhagen years, he did manage to impress a critical mass with his poetry and storytelling, and from this critical mass he won over a number of benefactors who would sponsor his education and early career. One of his earliest supporters and benefactors was Her Royal Highness, Crown Princess Caroline of Denmark.

Even powerful friends, however, were not enough to achieve the sort of immediate fame Andersen craved, so he promoted himself. To combat critical reviews at home in Denmark, Andersen sought a broader audience. He courted international approval by sending his published works along with letters of personal introduction to famous authors in other countries. This clever maneuver resulted in his being, for a time, more famous abroad than at home. Andersen's story "The Nightingale" tells of a plain bird, born to sing, that is internationally famous but virtually unknown at home. It was a story close to Andersen's heart.

Andersen remained a bachelor his entire life. He asserted that he fell in love twice, both times with women he hardly knew and with whom he never became romantically involved. He also had several male crushes throughout his life; however, it seems that none of these infatuations progressed to the status of an adult relationship. For the man who could so adeptly win the minds and hearts of children seems to have never, himself, officially left his childhood behind.

THE ANDERSEN STATUE

ARTIST Johannes Gelert (1852–1923)*

DATE September 26, 1896

BENEFACTOR American citizens of Danish descent throughout the country

LOCATION East of Stockton Drive, just north of Armitage Avenue

PARTICULARS Eight-foot-high bronze atop a ten-foot-plus pedestal of solid Minnesota granite

More than $10,000 was raised from Danes across the country to erect a statue celebrating their most illustrious countryman, the storyteller Hans Christian Andersen. Money was collected piecemeal, in tiny donations. In October 1891, the monument fund was launched by the Dania Society of Chicago, when twelve hundred Chicago Danes each contributed fifteen cents following the announcement of a proposed sculpture. Thereafter, the bulk of the fund was raised from children nationwide donating pennies and nickels.

The commission for a bronze likeness was awarded to Danish-American sculptor Johannes Gelert. The Chicago-based artist created a clay model of a seated Andersen, and from the clay rendition the bronze was cast in Chicago. In describing his work, Gelert explained, "I have tried to represent Andersen as he was about twenty years before his death. . . . In catching the expression of the face I have had the advantage of studying several good photographs of Andersen, taken at various times in his life."[42]

Gelert poetically portrayed the Danish author sitting outside on a tree stump, gazing out over imaginary water. Andersen is depicted in a contemplative mood, taking a break from reading his book. Nearby, a swan, with raised wings, reminds the viewer of Andersen's beloved story "The Ugly Duckling," which Andersen wrote as a metaphor for his own fairy-tale life.

Although the statue was originally intended to be in its place by the time of the 1893 Chicago World's Fair, it was not until the windy, rain-threatening afternoon of September 26, 1896, that Gelert's creation was unveiled before a crowd of ten thousand. The statue's finished presentation included a solid

---

* Johannes Gelert also created the Grant statue in Galena, IL; the Haymarket monument in Chicago; and the stolen Beethoven bust that once graced Lincoln Park.

pedestal of Minnesota granite, apparently in recognition of the considerable support received from Minnesota Danes.

On the day of the unveiling, festivities began with a procession, including many Danish societies, which gathered at Michigan Avenue and Adams Street and then marched north to the statue's Lincoln Park location, near where Armitage Avenue meets the park. Crowds who arrived at the ceremony early found the statue covered with the Danish and American flags. Children from nearby public schools, including the Hans Christian Andersen Public School, were in attendance.

During the presentation, which included some lengthy speeches, the great mass of onlookers was charmed when a young woman neared the statue and tossed a wreath of flowers, which caught one of the statue's hands.

The celebration closed with the voices of schoolchildren leading the audience in singing "America."

KAUGUST

6

Friedrich von Schiller

GERMAN DRAMATIST AND POET
1759–1805

Stood I in Creation all alone,
Spirits I would dream into each stone,
And their forms with kisses then would greet,—
When my wailings echoed far and wide,
Would be happy, if the Rocks replied,
Fool, enough! to Sympathy so sweet.

(Friedrich von Schiller,
"The Philosophical Letters,"
"Theosophy of Julius—Love")*

riedrich von Schiller's work as a playwright and poet is beloved and esteemed for its humanist ideals. Schiller's writings depict a fervent love and respect for man's dignity and liberty. He explored themes of freedom: political freedom, spiritual freedom, freedom to determine one's own destiny, and the inward freedom of the soul.

Schiller was only twenty-two when he self-published his first drama, *The Robbers*, a tragedy that was both wildly popular and, in some places, banished. This story of evil brother against brother-turned-evil, with the father in the middle, entertained and shocked audiences with its great passion and startling action. Fans of the play identified with the brother-turned-evil protagonist who seeks to right the private wrongs he's been dealt by turning against society at large and living a life of retribution and vengeance. Critics of the play recoiled and expressed horror.†

---

* Schiller published "The Philosophical Letters" in the March 1786 edition of *Thalia*, Schiller's journal of poetry and philosophical writings.

† French Revolutionists named Schiller an honorary citizen for *The Robbers*. Such admiration, however, was unfounded, because the play's conclusion reveals the futility of terror and revolution and the supremacy of law and order. Furthermore, Schiller abhorred the progress of the French Revolution and at one point planned to write a defense of the French King, only to learn in short time of the regicide and that his words were too late.

Schiller was able to create an evil-doing, yet sympathetic protagonist because he himself was probably enraged at the time of the play's writing. Schiller wrote the bulk of *The Robbers* in the final year—a year he was forced to repeat—of his seven-year, oppressive military school education.

In the years following *The Robbers*, Schiller matured as a writer of drama and poetry, partly by throwing himself into the challenging pursuits of amateur historian and philosopher, and partly by living through and observing the revolutionary times in which he lived.*

With a keen interest in history and in man's quest for both personal and political freedom, Schiller would go on to create his best-known works, his passionate and serious historical dramas, *Don Carlos, Wallenstein, Mary Stuart, The Maid of Orleans,* and *Wilhem Tell.*[†]

In *Wallenstein,* his masterpiece, Schiller wrote of the century that preceded him and the destructive Thirty Years War, a war that pitted European Protestants against European Catholics and laid to waste huge tracts of primarily German-speaking land. Schiller presents the heroic and ambitious figure of Wallenstein, an enormously powerful nobleman who is beloved by his troops for his great courage and talent. Serving as a commander of the Catholic forces, Wallenstein considers changing sides, yet he cannot make up his mind.[‡] His indecision causes his downfall because time does not wait for him. With his inaction, Wallenstein inadvertently sets in motion a chain of events that tragically leads to his own murder. The seemingly all-powerful hero is in fact not free to determine his own destiny; rather, outside forces and time trap him in an inescapable snare.

Man thinks that he is free to do his deeds,
But no! He is the plaything of a blind
Unheeding force, that fashions what was choice
Swiftly into a grim necessity.

(Schiller, *The Death of Wallenstein,* Act IV, Scene 8)

---

* Schiller lived at the height of Europe's Age of Enlightenment, a period when yearnings for freedom and democracy helped fuel the American and French revolutions.

† These listed plays are loosely and respectively based on Prince Don Carlos of Spain, Commander Albrecht von Wallenstein of the Thirty Years War, Queen Mary Stuart of Scotland, Joan of Arc, and the Swiss liberation movement.

‡ Wallenstein is an excellent dramatic character as he is truly an enigmatic historical figure. Historians still debate whether Wallenstein was working with the other side in order to secure peace or whether he was a traitor working for his own aggrandizement.

Schiller's most masterful poetry reveals his philosophical mind and interest in aesthetics.* Some of his most consequential poetry addresses his belief that art is the prime civilizing agent in the world. With his love of freedom and his fervent wish for the progress of mankind, Schiller promoted through poetry the idea that art was a liberating, healing, and ennobling social force. Yet Schiller does not promote art as an escape from life's hardships. On the contrary, in one of his best-regarded poems, "The Ideal and Life," he celebrates a life of energetic, hard work as a necessary means to realizing a peaceful, harmonious existence.

> For never, save to toil untiring, spoke
> The unwilling truth from her mysterious well—
> The statue only to the chisel's stroke
> Wakes from its marble cell.

> But onward to the sphere of beauty—go
> Onward, O child of art! and, lo!
> Out of the matter which thy pains control
> The statue springs!—not as with labor wrung
> From the hard block, but as from nothing sprung—
> Airy and light—the offspring of the soul!
> The pangs, the cares, the weary toils it cost
> Leave not a trace when once the work is done—
> The Artist's human frailty merged and lost
> In art's great victory won!

> (Schiller, "The Ideal and Life," stanza 7, lines 7–10; stanza 8)

At age thirty-one, after years of loneliness, Schiller married Charlotte von Lengefeld. Their union was a happy one and produced four children. Tragically, however, after only eleven months of marriage, Schiller was struck with a debilitating illness that would plague him for the next fourteen years. Tuberculosis claimed his young, productive life before he reached his forty-sixth birthday.

---

* Aesthetics, in short, is a branch of philosophy concerned with understanding beauty, art, and taste.

THE SCHILLER STATUE

ARTIST Ernst Bildhauer Rau (1839–1875)

DATE May 15, 1886

BENEFACTOR Schwaben Verein and Chicago citizens of German descent

LOCATION Just east of where Stockton Drive meets Webster Avenue, outside the west entrance to Lincoln Park Zoo

PARTICULARS Ten-foot-high bronze atop pedestal made of granite from Quincy, Massachusetts

The unveiling of the statue honoring the German dramatist and poet Friedrich von Schiller was fittingly surrounded by some rather dramatic circumstances. Minorly melodramatic was the heavy rain and sleet that set in at the ceremony's commencement, but the crowd of more than seven thousand was not discouraged. The onlookers, mostly of German descent, were eager to participate in the dedication that had already been postponed a week. The initial date of Saturday, May 8, was only four days after the infamous Chicago Haymarket riot, and in those first days following, all large gatherings were banned.*

When Chicago Mayor Carter Harrison spoke at the Schiller monument dedication, he did not fail to relate Schiller's ideas to Chicago's recent turmoil. His words were received with loud applause when he expounded:

> I wish simply to say that if all the German-speaking people to whom Schiller has been such a blessing had only read well and weighed his words we would possibly a few nights ago not have seen that dread scene that was enacted on Haymarket square. Schiller loved liberty, but liberty with art. He loved liberty, but he loved liberty with law. Schiller fought for the liberty of free speech and free thought, but he wanted free thought to be always reined in and circumscribed by the rules of art. He wanted liberty, but liberty with law. . . . If the Anarchists and Nihilists, who would

---

* Sunday, May 9, 1886, the eighty-first anniversary of Schiller's death, was the initial intended date, but park commissioners worried that a Sunday would produce too large of a crowd and that the Lincoln Park gardens would be trampled and ruined for the summer. Therefore, Saturday, May 8, was first scheduled.

    The Haymarket affair of Tuesday, May 4, 1886, left seven police officers dead and sixty wounded, and injured an unknown number of civilians, assumed to be about equal in number to what the police suffered. The terror, which began with a bomb, was led by Chicago German-American anarchists who were rallying in support of striking workers.

destroy all law, would but listen to that [illegible] of Schiller then the Anarchist would disappear and law would rise in respect.[43]

The chairman of the Monument Committee, Julius Rosenthal, gave a speech in German. A translation of his words expressed his wish that "the monument would be a preacher to every observer, exhorting him to enter within himself from the noisy activity of the world and turn his thoughts from the narrow, selfish, everyday work to the ideals of humanity."[44]

After a Miss Lena Stüedli recited Schiller's poem "The Words of Belief," the crowd cheered, and the drape covering the statue was dropped. Mr. Rosenthal then officially presented the statue to the Park Board "as proof of the patriotism of the German-Americans."[45]

It was the Park Board that had chosen the sculpture's excellent site, which borders the southern end of Lincoln Park gardens. General Stockton, speaking for the Park Board, replied to Mr. Rosenthal at the ceremony, "In selecting the spot dedicated to the monument, the Commissioners took into consideration . . . that his statue should be placed where he himself would love to linger were he here with us today among the flowers, and where the birds love to come and sing. It seems to me, sir that he must have had in his own mind just such an occasion as this when he wrote these lines to the Obelisk:

On a pedestal lofty the sculptor in triumph has raised me.
'Stand thou,' spoke he, and I stand proudly and joyfully here."[46]

The idea for the Schiller statue came as a resolution in an 1880 meeting of the Schwaben Verein, originally a mutual-aid society for German immigrants. Over the next five years, the organization raised and saved money for the $3,200 statue plus an approximate additional $5,000 to defray the cost of its transport, its pedestal, and its erection.

The bronze was quite inexpensive, because it was a duplicate of an already existing statue in Marbach, Germany, Schiller's birthplace. German artist Ernst Bildhauer Rau had created this original Schiller likeness. Using the same mold as the Marbach statue, William Polargus cast Lincoln Park's copy in Stuttgart, Germany. The $3,700 pedestal was designed by Professor C. Dollinger of Stuttgart but was executed in Chicago.

For a time, Lincoln Park's Schiller statue was decorated annually on the writer's birthday, November 10, with wreaths and flowers, and records do exist for some of these honors. In 1909, on the 150th anniversary of Schiller's birth, a grand celebration was held by the Schwaben Verein of Chicago. The principal speaker was Congressman Henry S. Boutell, who knowledgeably articulated the essence of Schiller's work and influence. He said:

Schiller is well described as the poet of freedom. To some he is known chiefly as the herald of revolt against the ancient tyrannies that shackled the lives and thoughts of men.

But the freedom which Schiller would have mankind aspire to is something more than civil and religious liberty, something higher and nobler. It is the glorious freedom of the soul that each individual must win for himself by the conquest of unrighteousness. It is the freedom that is born of truth. . . .

It is not a mere fanciful conception that Schiller had had a direct influence upon the destiny of this nation. About the middle of the last century, many Germans who had taken a leading part in the revolution of 1848 found a refuge in the United States. Every one brought with him Schiller's poems in his pocket or in his memory, and Schiller's spirit of freedom in his soul.

It is fitting that this statue of the poet of freedom stand forever amid the trees and flowers of this garden of the people, which bears the name and shelters also the statue of freedom's bravest champion and noblest martyr.

Lincoln and Schiller were apostles of the same faith, and their influence will widen with the passing years. The republic that Lincoln saved will endure, because the freedom that Schiller taught will prevail, the freedom that both Lincoln and Schiller exemplified in their lives and work, the freedom of the soul which is righteousness of life.[47]

7

William Shakespeare

ENGLISH DRAMATIST AND POET

1564–1616

There's a divinity that shapes our ends,
Rough-hew then how we will.

Hamlet

*T*he world is fortunate that so much of William Shakespeare's work survives. Seven years after his death, two of his close associates published in one volume his thirty-six plays, half of which had never before appeared in print. Without the foresight of his colleagues, works such as *Julius Caesar*, *Macbeth*, *Antony and Cleopatra*, and *The Tempest* may never have been known. Many plays of this era by other playwrights met a very different fate: they were lost. Shakespeare, famous in his own lifetime, received different treatment from his contemporaries for they knew him to be "the wonder of our Stage" and the "Star of poets."[48]

Shakespeare was enormously productive in his lifetime, as a part owner of a theater company, the Lord Chamberlain's Men; as one of its actors; and of course as a principal writer. Helping to run the business of the company by day, he probably went home after a full day's work to do much of his research and writing at night. And he didn't just write plays. Shakespeare also left behind 154 sonnets and two narrative poems. His most famous sonnet is about the enduring power of poetry and begins, "Shall I compare thee to a summer's day?"

To pursue his theater career, Shakespeare moved to London sometime in his mid- to late-twenties, leaving behind a wife and three young children. Shakespeare would live apart from his family for nearly twenty years, only seeing them on visits, and was probably away from home, unable to return in time, before his young son Hamnet died at age eleven. When he retired and returned to his hometown of Stratford-upon-Avon, he seemed desirous of returning to a life of ordinariness and of enjoying some extended time with his two daughters and one granddaughter. He, however, was probably not returning to his wife,

Anne Hathaway, although there is no certainty of this. The few known facts of their marriage are that they married when he was eighteen and she was twenty-six and pregnant; they lived apart for the bulk of their marriage; and in his will, the wealthy, retired Shakespeare made only one provision for his wife: "Item I gyve vnto my wife my second best bed with the furniture."[49]

Shakespeare wrote to sell tickets, to entertain the common man as well as his queen or king and their court. To appeal to his diverse audience and probably to express and make sense of his own life experiences, he loaded his plays with themes for all tastes, enduring themes such as honor, marriage, rebellion, desire, death, relinquishing power, betrayal, and forgiveness, and this is a short list. Perhaps even better, he laced his works with moments of humor and memorable characters.

Shakespeare's greatest gift, a gift that no other writer of the English language has surpassed, was his genius-level language ability. A man who was probably the first in his family to be able to sign his own name went on to write countless memorable lines that are today our catchphrases. "To thine own self be true," "neither a borrower nor a lender be," "in my mind's eye," and "it was Greek to me," are just a few. Shakespeare must have absorbed words and must have had a remarkable memory. And when English failed to provide all the words he needed, he simply made up new ones. Yet all of his plays, sonnets, and poems apparently fail to fully exhibit Shakespeare's verbal acumen, for the men who first thought to compile a complete volume of Shakespeare's work added to this collection a brief but intriguing biographical statement. They remembered, "What he thought, he uttered with that easiness that we have scarce received from him a blot in his papers."[50]

THE SHAKESPEARE STATUE

ARTIST	William Ordway Partridge (1861–1930)
DATE	April 23, 1894
BENEFACTOR	Samuel Johnston (1833–1886)
LOCATION	East of intersection at W. Belden Avenue and N. Lincoln Park West
PARTICULARS	Seven-and-a-half-foot-high bronze, atop a low pedestal

On April 23, 1894, a crowd gathered in Lincoln Park to witness the unveiling of the William Shakespeare statue. April 23 was particularly meaningful because it is not only the date celebrated as the bard's birthday, but it is also the date on which he died.

A description of the affair tells of long lines of carriages and a crowd of onlookers several hundred feet deep, in all directions. Miss Cornelia Williams, grandniece of the deceased benefactor, Samuel Johnston, dropped the drape covering the statue with a tug on a cord.

Cincinnati-born Samuel Johnston graduated from Harvard University and thereafter settled in Chicago, where he invested in real estate and was, for a time, a director of the cable car company, Chicago City Railroad Company. Upon Johnston's death in October of 1886, his will provided $10,000 for the creation of a bronze Shakespeare statue for Lincoln Park. With this memorial, Johnston's wish was to show his affection for Chicago. His will also left $10,000 for a gate at the entrance of Harvard University's college yard; $10,000 for the Cincinnati Orphan Asylum; $50,000 for St. Luke's Hospital; and $25,000 for the Chicago Nursery and Half Orphan Asylum. William E. Furness, one of the trustees of Johnston's will, described Johnston at the statue's unveiling as an educated man but not especially a man of literature.

In the spring of 1889, the trustees of Johnston's will sent letters to important sculptors worldwide, inviting them to submit models for a Lincoln Park Shakespeare statue competition. Numerous artists replied, some with models, some with photos and even a few with mere letters touting their reputations. In February of 1890, the committee awarded William Ordway Partridge the commission based on his model, which was about three feet high.

Partridge, twenty-eight when he won the commission, was born in Paris to American parents. His father was an amateur artist, and his cousin, John Rogers, was a respected sculptor. Partridge attended Columbia University in New York City and was multitalented, having spent time in the theater, having written several volumes of poetry, and, of course, having studied sculpture with notable artists in Paris, Florence, and Rome. He expressed his excitement about the commission: "All the literary work and all the study of my life have led up to the conception and execution of this Shakespearean statue. My stage experience and my intellectual associations with Shakespearean scholars have gradually given me a grasp of the subject, the perfection of artistic conception. This Shakespeare has been in my mind for years. I have turned it about from point to point, completing or changing its details one by one. It is the work of my life."[51]

Depicting Shakespeare's likeness was a puzzle because no portraits were done during his lifetime, or at least none survive. The two portraits that are considered genuine were done posthumously, within the first seven years after his death. Although Partridge thoroughly examined 137 Shakespeare depictions, he put his faith in only three: the death mask and the first two "genuine" renditions—a bust that overlooks the poet's grave and an engraving created for the publication of the first complete collection of Shakespeare's plays. Based on this research, Partridge next created fifteen studies just of the head.

For the bard's clothes, Partridge had a costume constructed by the wardrobe designer of Sir Henry Irving, an English Shakespearian actor. Partridge was very proud that his statue was the first dressed in historically correct garb.

Sitting on a low pedestal, the seated Shakespeare is inviting for children who often will climb up to sit on his lap. The poet looks to be caught in a daydream, focused on his mind's eye, holding his book aside, page marked with a finger. On the front of the base a quote from *Hamlet* reads, "What a piece of work is man! how noble in reason! how infinite in faculty!" Engraved on the back of the base is a quote by English poet Samuel T. Coleridge. It reads, "He was not for an age but for all time, our myriad-minded Shakespeare."

For the World's Fair of 1893, a plaster model of Partridge's Shakespeare was on exhibit at the Fine Arts Building, today our Museum of Science and Industry. Partridge intended to have the bronze version present, but it is unclear whether or not it arrived in time from Paris, where it was cast. If it didn't make it, Partridge could not have been too unhappy, because his collection of sculptures was apparently the largest at the Fair.*

At the dedication ceremony in Lincoln Park the following year, Partridge expressed: "A sculptor speaks best in bronze and marble, yet it may please you to know how I put three years of work on this statue. I cannot tell you the story of it; it was a labor of love."[52]

---

* Other sculptures by Partridge on exhibit at the Fair included a statue of Alexander Hamilton, heads of J.R. Lowell, E.E. Hale, Christ, Mary, and an old withered woman titled "Nearing Home." Notable sculptures by Partridge later in his career include General Grant in 1896 for the Union League Club of Brooklyn; Pocahontas in 1921 for Jamestown, Virginia; and a Jefferson statue to join his Hamilton statue at Columbia University of New York.

KAUGUST

8

Alexander Hamilton

AMERICA'S FIRST SECRETARY OF THE TREASURY
1755–1804

To be able to borrow upon *good terms*, it is essential that the credit of a nation should be well established. . . .
. . . by good faith, by a punctual performance of contracts. States, like individuals, who observe their engagements, are respected and trusted: while the reverse is the fate of those, who pursue an opposite conduct.

Alexander Hamilton, *Report on Public Credit, January 9, 1790* [53]

Alexander Hamilton was one of our most controversial founding fathers, so much so that even in death, he has often not received due respect. Hamilton sparked controversy with his bold, visionary work as our nation's first treasury secretary, work that laid the foundation for generations of prosperity.

From the Caribbean island of Nevis, Hamilton immigrated to the states at age seventeen and rose to the top echelons of power remarkably fast. After joining a volunteer militia at age twenty, it would take him just two years to earn the position of General Washington's right-hand man in the Revolutionary War. And from that point on, he was forever in the thick of our nation's rise.

Hamilton's list of accomplishments and contributions is not brief. He was a hero in battle, a fierce abolitionist, a practicing lawyer. He served as an elected delegate to a number of assemblies, most notably the Constitutional Convention. Throughout his life he wrote tirelessly, contributing essays and resolutions to papers of the day, vigorously putting forth his ideas for our budding nation. Hamilton was our first treasury secretary, and in this role, with a President who was sympathetic to his views, was effectively the second most powerful man in the nation, advising President Washington on foreign policy as well as treasury matters. And when Washington surrendered the highest office after serving two terms, it was Hamilton he asked to draft the bulk of his farewell address.

From his massive collection of writings, Hamilton's most consequential work was his conceiving, organizing, and coauthoring of the *Federalist Papers.** Writing to defend and promote the proposed U.S. Constitution, Hamilton worked at a feverish pace, writing twenty-one consecutive essays in just two months and ultimately, writing fifty-one of the eighty-five papers. Today the *Federalist Papers* continue to be a primary source for constitutional interpretation.

Hamilton's most masterful work, however, would come out of his service as our nation's first secretary of the treasury. In the financially precarious years following the war, Hamilton worked to establish the nation on sound financial footing by centralizing the country's fiscal affairs. Hamilton trumped states' powers with new and controversial federal powers.† A few years later, the executive branch of government changed hands, and Anti-Federalist Thomas Jefferson became the third U.S. President. Jefferson ordered his own secretary of the treasury to conduct an in-depth appraisal of Hamilton's work, in order to uncover, in his words, "the blunders and frauds of Hamilton." This new secretary of the treasury tackled the task "with a very good appetite," and when he reported back to President Jefferson he confessed, "I have found the most perfect system ever formed. Any change that should be made in it would injure it. Hamilton made no blunders, committed no frauds. He did nothing wrong."[54]

Because he understood the complex issues of and the need for a financially strong central government, so soon after the country had fought off imperialist Britain, Hamilton proved to be a financial prodigy. While his supporters held him in awe for his visionary work, his foes, still reeling from tyrannical British rule, loathed and feared Hamilton's programs, viciously calling him a monarchist. There was irony, however, in these attacks. The self-made Hamilton was vilified for his capitalist visions primarily by southern, aristocratic slaveholders who believed a strong central government threatened their southern agrarian society based on slavery.

While Hamilton was not the monarchist that his foes claimed, he was a proponent of a strong central government, fearing that a nation of loosely held states could too easily succumb to mob rule. In the tenuous years following the

---

* Author Ron Chernow humorously guessed that Hamilton "must have produced the maximum number of words that a human being can scratch out in forty-nine years." Chernow, *Hamilton,* 5.

† As treasury secretary, Hamilton established a central bank, raised taxes, devised a tariff system, and aggregated state debt. There were no land or income taxes at this time, so "raised taxes" refers to the unpopular liquor tax that Hamilton enacted, also known as the whiskey tax.

revolution, Hamilton's deepest concern was to construct a government for this new union in which liberty was balanced with order. He wrote, "As too much power leads to despotism, too little leads to anarchy, and both eventually to the ruin of the people."[55, *]

Hamilton married Eliza Schuyler, with whom he had eight children. Hamilton was imperfect as a husband, subjecting the young nation to its first major sex scandal.[†] Still, Eliza was steadfastly devoted to Hamilton in his lifetime and to Hamilton's legacy in the fifty years of her widowhood, dying in 1854 at age ninety-seven.

Hamilton left us by route of the greatest political drama in our nation's early history. He was mortally shot in a duel with one of his political foes, vice president of the United States, Aaron Burr.[‡]

Hamilton's premature and senseless death at age forty-nine shocked and depressed his admirers. Our country's preeminent financial genius, however, ironically left his family in financial distress. Despite all the accusations throughout his lifetime of his personally benefiting from his political position, Hamilton never once profited from his work, and unlike founding fathers Washington, Jefferson, and Madison, he cut off all outside sources of income while in office. When he left office, his assets consisted primarily of household furniture, and his debts amounted to years of future work. For Hamilton was not driven by money; rather his heart was first and foremost with his country.[§] Even on his deathbed, his mind focused for a time on the nation's uncertain future when he spoke some of his final words; he said, "If they break this union, they will break my heart."[56]

---

[*] Hamilton's childhood in the unruly West Indies attuned him, perhaps more than any other founding father, to the risks of anarchy.

[†] At age thirty-six, Hamilton began an affair with the twenty-three-year-old, married Maria Reynolds. The affair lasted nearly a year, and ultimately it was a means for Mr. and Mrs. Reynolds to blackmail the treasury secretary. It is unknown whether blackmail was the initial goal when Mrs. Reynolds first went to introduce herself to Hamilton at his home.

[‡] Hamilton threw away his shot in the duel. His strategy was to show the opponent no intention to kill while still not compromising honor by refusing to duel.

[§] When practicing law in the private sector, Hamilton was known for charging reasonable fees and for avoiding costly lawsuits by seeking arbitration or settlements.

THE HAMILTON STATUE

ARTIST	John Angel (1881–1960)
DATE	1941, unveiled July 6, 1952
BENEFACTOR	Kate Sturges Buckingham (1857–1937)
LOCATION	East of Wrightwood Avenue and Lincoln Park West intersection
PARTICULARS	Thirteen-foot-high bronze, coated with gold leaf, atop an eight-foot-high red granite base

Kate Sturges Buckingham's last-realized gift to Chicago was a $1 million appropriation set aside in 1928 for the designing, sculpture, and maintenance of an Alexander Hamilton statue. Miss Buckingham wanted the statue to be situated in Grant Park between the Art Institute and Buckingham Fountain, her best-known gift to Chicago. Any residue from this handsome sum was to belong to the Art Institute.

Had Miss Buckingham's wish been granted, then it would have been the second Hamilton statue in Grant Park. She saw no obstacle in this, however, because she believed that history had not adequately given Hamilton the accolades he so deserved.

On July 6, 1952, in Lincoln Park, the Hamilton statue was finally unveiled before fifteen hundred onlookers, which included three descendants of Hamilton. Hamilton's great-great-grandson, Brigadier General Pierpont M. Hamilton of the U.S. Air Force and holder of the Congressional Medal of Honor, cut the ribbon at the opening of the ceremony.

With the words of Republican Senator Everett McKinley Dirksen, Hamilton's contributions were remembered and honored. Dirksen recalled that Hamilton "rolled up a scroll of accomplishments almost unmatched by any American I can name." He continued, "It was Hamilton who laid on the table of the convention a complete plan of national government. It became a structure on which the delegates could build. No one else has made such a contribution to the Constitution of the United States of America. But it still had to be accepted and ratified by the people, and it remained for him to make it possible."[57]

The thirteen-foot-tall bronze was completed in 1941 by English-born sculptor John Angel and was stored for more than ten years while it awaited a home. The project was seriously delayed for two reasons. For one, trustees of Buckingham's monies halted all work during the war years so as not to divert manpower and materials from the war effort. The park district additionally delayed the effort by taking more than twenty years to select a site.

The statue itself was created at a cost of $12,000, so there remained the considerable sum of $988,000 to finish the project, although a certain amount of this was intended for future maintenance. This attractive amount perhaps contributed to the project's delay. Grant Park commissioners stalled the undertaking by refusing to offer a site for the statue unless some of the money was also used to help construct a music arena. Monument trustees were hardly in a position to negotiate because five months before Miss Buckingham's death on December 14, 1937, she had declined this same proposal replying, "My idea was a simple monument to the man [Hamilton]—nothing else."[58]

Amazingly, the final cost of the venture amounted to nearly $550,000. Architects Marx, Flint & Schonne of Chicago created an elaborate memorial that no longer stands today. The original presentation included a three-level plaza of Indiana limestone and polished black and red granite. The statue sat directly upon a twenty-six ton base of blood-red granite, which stood eight feet high. It took three attempts to successfully quarry this block from Cold Springs, Minnesota. The statue itself was then gilded in twenty-four-karat gold leaf. Behind the golden statue, a contrasting polished black granite pylon soared to a height of seventy-eight feet.

In 1993, the memorial was considerably downsized. The three-level plaza and the pylon were removed. Today, the gold-leaf-covered statue is simply presented atop its original red granite monolith.

Kate Sturges Buckingham inherited her wealth from her family. Her mother's father, Solomon Sturges, built Chicago's first grain elevator. Her father, Ebenezer Buckingham also built grain elevators and in later years was involved in insurance and banking enterprises. Her father left his fortune to his three children upon his death in 1912, and Kate was the sole survivor by 1920.

Kate's family moved to Chicago in 1858 when she was just a year old, and she would grow up to be a major benefactor—most often anonymously—to the fine arts in Chicago. Recipients of her generosity included the Art Institute, countless Chicago charities, unnamed Chicagoans, and more than two hundred music and art students. In 1927, Miss Buckingham paid for the building of the Buckingham Fountain as a memorial to her dear brother Clarence. Upon her death at age seventy-nine, she left $50,000 for a children's playground, some funds to friends and employees, and the remainder of her estate, approximately $4 million, to the Art Institute. She was buried in Zanesville, Ohio, the place of her birth.

KAUGUST

9

Johann Wolfgang von Goethe

GERMAN DRAMATIST, NOVELIST, POET

1749–1832

Unfettered spirits will aspire in vain
To the pure heights of perfection.
He who wills great things must gird up his loins;
only in limitation is mastery revealed,
and law alone can give us freedom.

(Johann Wolfgang von Goethe, excerpt from "Nature and Art"[59])

ohann Wolfgang von Goethe is regarded as one of the great minds of Western civilization, and he ranks with Shakespeare and Dante for his literary genius and output. He remarkably contributed masterpieces to every genre of writing, and he composed a staggering quantity of work, enough to fill twenty to thirty generously sized volumes. Do the titles *Faust, The Sorrows of Young Werther,* or *Wilhem Meister's Apprenticeship* ring a bell?

At twenty-four, Goethe became an instant celebrity when he published the novel *The Sorrows of Young Werther.* The story of Werther, written as a series of letters, is that of a lovesick young man whose unchecked emotions drive him to take his own life. Werther's tragedy was partly autobiographical: Goethe confessed that he shot his hero "to escape from the waters of death."[60] Werther and Goethe both shared the same birthday (August 28) and both fell in love with a beautiful but engaged girl (Werther with Lotte and Goethe with Charlotte). The book achieved international cult-like status. Fans throughout Europe began to dress like Werther, and according to popular myth, there followed in Europe numerous copycat suicides. Later in life, Goethe regretted making so public early episodes from his private life.

Goethe had many talents and interests in addition to his literary work. He was schooled in seven languages, studied law, worked as a statesman, researched plant morphology, and dabbled in music. Early in his professional life he considered devoting himself to painting; in his later years he considered his writings about color theory to be perhaps his greatest legacy.

Faust, Goethe's supreme literary accomplishment, was started in his early twenties and finished in his eighty-third year, the year of his death. Written as a two-part dramatic poem, *Faust* is a complex story of an exceptionally learned and hubristic man who suffers because, for him, life is "destitute of pleasure." Desperate to be saved from life's "weary dance," Faust sells his soul to the devil. Faust's deal with the devil, not surprisingly, has tragic consequences, yet ultimately the story is one of redemption. In the end, Faust's soul is saved by the heavens with the words of angels: "He who strives on and lives to strive / Can earn redemption still."[61]

At age fifty-seven, Goethe married Christiane Vulpius, his longtime companion and the mother of his sixteen-year-old son, Karl August.

Goethe is often quoted today because he authored numerous Confucian-like sayings. Here are some favorites:

The first and last thing demanded of genius is love of truth.

(Maxims and Reflections, 382)

For surely everyone only hears what he understands.

(Maxims und Reflections, 887)[62]

What should the solving of Nature's secrets be? The discovery of God both within and without.

(Selected Verse)[63]

THE GOETHE STATUE

ARTIST	Hermann Hahn (1868–1944)
DATE	June 13, 1914
BENEFACTOR	Schwaben Verein and German-American residents of Chicago
LOCATION	Near Diversey Parkway, Lakeview Avenue, and Lagoon Drive intersection
PARTICULARS	Twenty-five-foot-high bronze

Twenty thousand spectators gathered to celebrate the unveiling of the Goethe bronze on June 13, 1914. The crowd, mostly Chicagoans of German descent and representing some fifty German organizations, participated in the three-hour ceremony despite the drizzling rain.

The idea for a Goethe statue in Chicago had been brewing for some twenty-five years. Schwaben Verein, originally a mutual-aid society for emigrants from Schwaben in Germany, organized and raised nearly $50,000 for the project. To select an artist, an international competition was held, and nine artists submitted work.* In 1910, at the Royal Academy of the Arts in Berlin, an international jury unanimously named forty-two-year-old Hermann Hahn of Munich, Germany, the competition winner.† The other favored model was a temple design by Hugo Lederer, but it was considered too expensive.

Hahn created a symbolic statue to honor Goethe's life and work—reportedly Lincoln Park commissioners had stipulated no additional portrait statues. The statue shows a confident, youthful, athletic male wearing a cape and standing with an eagle. Interpretation? Perhaps you see a heroic German figure, with the cape indicating hero and the eagle being read as a longtime symbol of Germany. Others may see a godlike figure, because Zeus, king of the gods, is often symbolized with an eagle.

The base of the statue reads *Mastermind of the German People*. A low wall behind the sculpture features an excerpt from *Faust* inscribed in German and English:

> The last result of wisdom stamps it true:
> He only earns his freedom and existence,
> Who daily conquers them anew.
> Thus here, by dangers girt, shall glide away
> Of childhood, manhood, age, the vigorous day:
> And such a throng I fain would see,—
> Stand on free soil among a people free!

Following the ceremony, a banquet was held at the Germania Club‡ honoring special guests Herman Hahn and Professor Hugo Münsterberg of Harvard University. Professor Münsterberg's speech on that night celebrated the contributions of German immigrants, whom he at one point referred to as "the non-English elements of the people." He elaborated, "Hence the true duty of every American is to contribute to the new nation the noblest and ripest which he can bring from his native land."[64]

---

* All nine submitted models were later brought to Chicago for a special exhibit in January 1911 at the Art Institute.

† Much of Herman Hahn's work was in Germany and was of 19th century Germans (Moltke, Liszt, Max Schillings) and architectural sculpture.

‡ The building Germania Place, built in 1888 by architect August Fiedler, still stands in Old Town.

10

Philip Henry Sheridan

AMERICAN GENERAL
1831–1888

I do not believe war to be simply that lines should engage each other in battle and therefore do not regret the system of living on the enemy's country. These men or women did not care how many were killed, or maimed, so long as war did not come to their doors, but as soon as it did come in the shape of loss of property, they earnestly prayed for its termination. As war is a punishment, if we can, by reducing its advocates to poverty, end it quicker, we are on the side of humanity.[65]

General Phil Sheridan, 1864[*]

Hurrah! hurrah for Sheridan!
Hurrah! hurrah for horse and man!
And when their statues are placed on high
Under the dome of the Union sky,
The American soldier's Temple of Fame,
There, with the glorious general's name,
Be it said, in letters both bold and bright:
"Here is the steed that saved the day
By carrying Sheridan into the fight,
From Winchester—twenty miles away!"

(Thomas Buchanan Read, "Sheridan's Ride," stanza 7)

"Sheridan's Ride" was written within weeks of General Philip Sheridan's famous ride to overturn a near-lost battle against Confederate soldiers on October 19, 1864. The poem captured the hearts and imagination of a war-weary

---

[*] Sheridan wrote this explanation in defense of the practice of pillaging civilians who housed and supported rebel fighters.

North, three-and-one-half years into a civil war that had no end in sight.[*] In that election year, Republicans exploited Read's patriotic words to help secure Abraham Lincoln's reelection, which was highly unlikely only two months earlier. And for some fifty years following the Civil War, northern school children recited "Sheridan's Ride," securing Philip Sheridan's fame for generations.

Read's minor poetic achievement celebrates Sheridan's seemingly miraculous victory at Cedar Creek. On the morning of the battle, Sheridan was returning to his men from Washington, DC, where he had met with the secretary of war. From about twelve miles away, the sounds of battle alerted Sheridan and his companions, and after putting his ear to the ground, Sheridan understood that the Union army was retreating. As they rode toward the battleground, Sheridan and his party encountered hundreds of fleeing Union soldiers, some injured. Supply wagons and ambulances encountered along the way blocked Sheridan's movement to the front. Sheridan surveyed the beaten soldiers, many of whom were beaten only in spirit, and quickly resolved to go forward to fight. "Come on back, boys!" he shouted. "Give 'em hell, God damn 'em! We'll make coffee out of Cedar Creek tonight!" He continued, "Come on back! Face the other way. We're going to lick those fellows out of their boots!"[66] And he spurred his horse, Rienzi, on to the battleground.

Union soldiers cheered Sheridan's return to the front, and quickly their confidence returned. Sheridan assessed the battlefield and swiftly set to organizing a counterattack. To rally his men, he rode his horse across the length of the front, waving his hat in his right hand. The aggressive Sheridan had the special ability to instill optimism and resolve in his soldiers with his presence.

And beat them back they did. Under Sheridan's direction, the Rebels soon gave up the short-lived certainty of their advance. Four days later, Lincoln thanked Sheridan with yet another promotion. At age thirty-three, Sheridan became a major general.

Six months later, in the Civil War's final battle at Appomattox, it was Sheridan's men who relentlessly pursued General Lee, with Sheridan anticipating most of Lee's moves. When word reached Sheridan that Lee had finally surrendered, Sheridan was in the midst of planning a counterattack and grumbled, "Damn them. I wish they had held out an hour longer and I would have

---

[*] The American Civil War, April 12, 1861, to April 9, 1865, was the costliest war in American history in terms of American casualties. Approximately 620,000 Union and Confederate soldiers died, more than the combined totals of World War I, World War II, and the Korean War.

whipped hell out of them." He clenched his fist and added, "I've got 'em like that!"[67]

Phil Sheridan was a career army man who dealt with the time's toughest challenges, war or no war. After the Civil War, Sheridan would go on to manage Reconstruction in Texas and Louisiana, and thereafter, he took on the responsibility of controlling or accommodating the Indians of the Great Plains. Both jobs were highly complex, controversial, political, and dangerous.

It is difficult and sad to read about the American Indian struggles of this time period and stories of U.S. Army men fighting the various western Indian tribes. It is tempting to judge the many men like Sheridan who worked to protect white settlers from the indigenous people. Roy Morris, author of *Sheridan: The Life and Wars of General Phil Sheridan,* ultimately concludes, "Still, given the changing conditions on the post-Civil War frontier and the lack of a firm national consensus on the question of the Indians and their place in white dominated society, the army regulars under Sheridan had performed about as well as could have been expected in such a thankless and perilous job."[68]

At age forty-four, Sheridan married twenty-two-year-old Irene Rucker. Love visibly softened the lifelong soldier, and he happily became a father four times over.

After successfully completing his duties out West, which meant that the Indians were for the most part subdued, Sheridan was stationed in Chicago and lived on South Michigan Avenue.* In Chicago at the time of the fire (1871), Sheridan played several roles throughout the crisis. During the fire, he and his men worked in the Loop to contain the conflagration and stop it from moving south. In the fire's aftermath, Sheridan used his authority to maintain martial law and to organize relief efforts for the thousands of homeless citizens congregating in Lincoln Park.†

Sheridan developed health problems early, due perhaps in part to the stressful and physically demanding life he had led. At fifty-seven, he suffered his first heart attack, two months after touring the then proposed site of Fort Sheridan, north of Chicago.‡ A stunned Congress quickly voted to honor him with the

---

* From 1869 to 1883, Sheridan was temporarily stationed in Chicago where he served as commander of the Military Division of the Missouri.

† The Chicago Fire of October 8, 1871, raged for thirty-six hours and burnt to the ground a third of the city. Nearly a third of the citizens were left homeless. Sheridan lost all personal and professional papers in the fire. His house was saved, but his favorite horse, Breckinridge, his replacement mount in the Battle at Cedar Creek, was a casualty.

‡ Fort Sheridan was so named to honor Sheridan's services to Chicago.

rank of four-star general, which generals Grant and Sherman had previously been awarded. Sheridan would never fully recover and died of another massive heart attack three months later at his new vacation home, which he would never enjoy, in Nonquitt, Massachusetts.

THE SHERIDAN STATUE

ARTIST   Gutzon Borglum (1867–1941)
DATE   July 16, 1924
BENEFACTOR Illinois state legislature and private donations
LOCATION   Overlooking the intersection of Belmont Ave. and Sheridan Rd.
PARTICULARS Sixteen-foot-high bronze

Charles Tyson Yerkes, the businessman scoundrel who built Chicago's world-class transportation system, first conceived the idea for a Sheridan statue shortly after the general's death in 1888. Yerkes offered $50,000 for a bronze of Sheridan on horseback to be placed in Union Park, a small park just west of the Loop. Chicago's "Cable Czar" planned to depict Sheridan's famous ride to save the battle at Cedar Creek, and he intended to have the rendition in place in time for Chicago's World's Fair of 1893. His plan, however, was never realized. The notion was dropped after years of setbacks and after the World's Fair deadline had passed.*

The unpopular and distrusted Yerkes faced opposition to his Sheridan statue plan from Chicagoans. Initially, the public disapproved, for patriotic reasons, of the Parisian artist who was first awarded the commission. Public outcry grew so intense that the Parisian artist eventually abandoned the job after more than a year of work. In the months after, American artists submitted models; however, none was favored. One submission was ridiculed for depicting Sheridan's horse with all four feet off the ground. To one critic, the horse appeared to be "agonizingly impaled" on the "thin, broken tree" included to support the weight of the airborne steed and rider.[69]

---

* Yerkes was a transportation visionary who updated Chicago's inefficient transportation system with cable cars, electric trolleys, and elevated trains, including our beloved Loop train. The ex-convict from Philadelphia amassed an estimated $29 million through business thievery and bribery. Ultimately Yerkes left Chicago for New York and later London, where he worked on London's Underground transit system. Yerkes funded the University of Chicago's Yerkes Observatory located in William's Bay, Wisconsin, near Lake Geneva.

In June 1893, a second wealthy Chicagoan, W. T. Johnson, offered $50,000 for a Sheridan monument; however, Johnson stipulated that the city must offer a site at the head of Sheridan Road.* Nothing came of Johnson's offer, either.

More than twenty-five years later, after a Sheridan sculpture in Washington, DC, had been completed by artist Gutzon Borglum, Chicagoans finally resumed plans to erect a Sheridan statue, and Borglum was awarded the commission. Idaho-born Borglum is best known for his monumental presidents' heads at Mount Rushmore, South Dakota, and for the head of Lincoln in the national Capitol that he carved directly from the block of marble. Gutzon Borglum studied art in San Francisco and in Paris, where he interacted with and was influenced by sculptor Auguste Rodin.[†]

The president of the Sheridan Monument Committee, Michael J. Faherty, raised $50,000, collecting equal parts private and public monies. A site overlooking Sheridan Road at Belmont Avenue was appropriately selected.

Borglum's Chicago Sheridan rendering was similar to his Washington, DC, depiction. At the unveiling ceremony on July 16, 1924, Borglum described how he sought to capture Sheridan's famous ride from Winchester to Cedar Creek. For his work, he visualized Sheridan reining in his horse as he called encouraging words to retreating soldiers.

The monument ceremony took place on a hot, sunny day, with hundreds of infantrymen and artillerymen standing at attention. Sheridan's widow, Irene, and daughter, Mary Sheridan, were special guests of honor, and the keynote speaker was Major General H. C. Hale. Daughter Mary unveiled the artwork when she pulled the cord to drop the draping flag. A crowd of some ten thousand reacted with loud cheering, and military vessels on the lake, near Belmont, saluted with a seventeen-gun salute.

Ten years later, General Sheridan was once more officially celebrated, when admirers decorated his monument with a plaque. It reads:

> Philip H. Sheridan graduated from the United States Military Academy, West Point, July 1, 1853. To honor him and his alma mater, this tablet was placed here, by the Chicago Association of West Pointers, on September 19, 1934, the 70th anniversary of his victory in the battle of Opequan, Virginia.

---

* Johnson had served as Cook County treasurer and also as an Illinois state senator.

† Borglum also created the Lincoln Park portrait statue of Governor Altgeld, unveiled 1915.

11 & 12

American Indians

OF NORTHERN ILLINOIS

ative Americans inhabited the river basin region around Chicago for more than ten thousand years, until invading Iroquois* and later European settlers drove them out. Their history is largely unknown except for the years they shared their lands with early explorers, traders, and western settlers.

French explorers in the 1670s were the first outsiders to reach Illinois country, and they earned the trust of indigenous tribes through persistent and tactical diplomacy.† In the 1680s, French and Indian alliances produced the foremost concentration of Indians in northern Illinois when René-Robert Cavelier, Sieur de La Salle established Fort St. Louis at Starved Rock. The vicinity of this protected site, ninety miles southwest of Chicago, became a safe haven for Indians, local and migrating tribes, who sought protection from invading Iroquois warriors.

The lands that became Chicago's lakefront and downtown were never hospitable sites for aboriginal tribes. Sand dunes, swamps, foul lakeside weather, and exposure to passersby contrasted to the sheltered, timber-rich, agricultural land that would make life possible. Archaeological evidence indicates that dozens of Indian villages existed in the greater Chicago area, in more protected environments along rivers and streams. River routes between Lake Michigan and the Illinois River were particularly attractive settlement sites in summer months when trade flourished.

Various Indian tribes inhabited northern Illinois country at various times. Local Indian tribes included Miami, Kaskaskia, Ottawa, Ojibwa, Shawnee, and Potawatomi Indians.‡ Villages were generally not purely a single tribe or, once Europeans arrived, race. Native Americans mixed with each other for a number

---

* Iroquois Indians from the northeast—primarily present-day upstate New York—attacked Great Lakes Indian tribes, killing many, burning villages, and in some cases driving Great Lakes tribes westward.

† French traders may have reached Illinois country before the 1670s, but if they did, they left no written records.

‡ When the French arrived in Illinois territory in the late 1600s, they encountered two Indian ethnic groups, the Illinois and the Miami. At this time, Illinois Indians consisted of as many as twelve tribes and inhabited lands of the central Mississippi River valley (lands in present-day Illinois, Iowa, Missouri, and Arkansas). Miami Indians controlled lands south and west of Lake Michigan. By the 1800s, Illinois Indian tribes had disappeared or merged to the point that only two Illinois tribes remained, the Kaskaskia and Peoria nations. Descendents of the Illinois nation today are the Peoria Indians of Oklahoma.

Other Chicago-area tribes migrated to northern Illinois from the north and east, often displaced by warring Iroquois tribes.

of reasons: captive taking, marriage, extended visits, war alliance, migration, survival from disease, and religious callings. Indigenous tribes also mixed with traders of European or African origin.

In 1833, Potawatomi Indians, the principal area landowners at the time, were forced into selling five million acres, west of Lake Michigan, to the United States government. In return, they received equal acreage west of the Mississippi and more than one million dollars worth of goods and provisions. Soon after 1837, they were forced from the state entirely.

Aside from land, Indian words are another conspicuous inheritance from the Native Americans. *Chicago* was derived from an Indian word meaning "place of native garlic." *Allium tricoccum,* also known as ramps, wild leek, or wild onion, once thrived along area river systems that consequently bore the same Indian name, *chicagoua.*

THE ALARM

ARTIST   John Joseph Boyle (1851–1917)

DATE   May 5, 1884

BENEFACTOR   Martin Ryerson (1818–1887)

LOCATION   East of the lakeside path, north of where Diversey Harbor meets the lake, north of *Signal of Peace*[*]

PARTICULARS   Life-sized bronze, six feet in height, atop a ten-foot-high pedestal. Visit www.lincolnparkstatues.com to view a historic photo depicting the male with a headpiece of feather forms, a large tomahawk, and a collar. These original details are missing due to vandalism.

Martin Ryerson left his boyhood home in New Jersey at age sixteen to seek his fortune out West, and for the remainder of his life, business success came seemingly easily to him. His first stops were Detroit and Grand Rapids, Michigan, where the young Martin created some wealth trading furs with the Indians. He next moved to Muskegon, Michigan, where he entered the lumber business. His firm, Ryerson & Morris, prospered and branched out to Kenosha, Wisconsin, and Chicago. After 1848, Mr. Ryerson made his home in Chicago

---

[*] In 1974, *The Alarm* was moved from its home of ninety years. Originally it stood within the confines of our present-day Lincoln Park Zoo but was moved when plans were made to build a primate house.

and would multiply his fortune with real estate investments made as early as 1876 in Chicago's downtown.

Martin Ryerson commemorated the Ottawa Indians with a gift of statuary to Lincoln Park. At a modest ceremony held May 5, 1884, before a group of one hundred spectators, including Colonel G. S. Hubbard, one of Chicago's oldest citizens, Mr. Ryerson presented the monument he commissioned:

> I have caused the construction of this statue to commemorate the Ottawa race of Indians, with whom I spent several years of my early manhood. While with them I saw much that was good and noble, and I looked upon them as my friends. There are but few white people now living who understand that race as I did half a century ago . . . I therefore hope . . . that this statue will serve to show posterity for all time to come the opinion in which some of his co-existent white men held the Indian.[70]

Mr. Ryerson commissioned the New York-born sculptor, John Boyle, in Paris, approximately one year prior. Mr. Boyle had studied art in Philadelphia and at the Ecole des Beaux Arts academy in Paris. The bronze was executed in Philadelphia.

The statue, titled *The Alarm,* depicts a group of four: a standing Indian male grasping his tomahawk, a seated woman with her child, and a wolf-like dog in a guarded stance. All members of the group appear to be alert to some imminent danger. The statue's pedestal is ornamented with four bas-reliefs depicting Ottawa customs and life. These scenes are titled "The Corn Dance," "The Peace Pipe," "Forestry," and "The Hunt."*

---

* At least three of the original marble reliefs were stolen. All four have since been replaced with granite bas-relief panels.

SIGNAL OF PEACE

ARTIST	Cyrus E. Dallin (1861–1944)
DATE	June 9, 1894
BENEFACTOR	Lambert Tree (1832–1910)
LOCATION	East of the lakeside path, just north of where Diversey Harbor meets the lake*
PARTICULARS	Thirteen-foot-high bronze, to the top of the spear, atop a granite pedestal

Signal of Peace portrays a Sioux Indian chief signaling peace with a raised upward-pointed spear topped with eagle feathers.[†] Cyrus E. Dallin created this masterpiece while studying sculpture in Paris, where it gained admittance to the Paris Salon exhibition of 1890 and earned the distinction of "mention honorable." Warriors and ponies from the Buffalo Bill show, on tour in Paris at the time, served as models for the form.[‡] Dallin later remembered:

> The origin of that statue goes back to my boyhood, to a day when I witnessed a peace pow-wow between the Indian chiefs and the United States Army officers. I shall never forget those splendid looking Indians arrayed in their gorgeous head-dress riding upon their ponies to the army camp. . . . In making my model of "Signal of Peace," I used, to a certain extent, one of the Buffalo Bill Indians; in putting into it that dignity typical of the Indian, I had in my memory the chiefs who rode up to the peace pow-wow many years before.[71]

In 1893 at the Chicago Columbian Exposition, *Signal of Peace* won a medal, a diploma, and a sale. Judge Lambert Tree purchased the award-winning statue with the intent of giving it to Lincoln Park.[§] On January 2, 1894, Judge Tree formally donated his acquisition with a letter that in part reads:

---

* The monument was originally located a short distance northwest of the General Grant statue.

† *Signal of Peace* would become the first in a series of permanent, life-sized Indian equestrian statues by Dallin. *Medicine Man* graces Fairmount Park, Philadelphia. *The Scout* stands in Kansas City, Missouri, and *Appeal to the Great Spirit* adorns the entrance to the Boston Museum of Fine Arts.

‡ The Buffalo Bill show was a touring circus-like show that by 1893 featured horse-culture groups including: U.S. and other military, American Indians, and others from all over the world.

§ In 1889, Judge Tree gave the René-Robert de La Salle statue to Lincoln Park. Judge Tree also built the Tree Studios (1894–1913), located in River North, to entice artists working at the 1893 World's Fair to remain in Chicago.

I fear that the time is not distant when our descendants will only know through the chisel and brush of the artist these simple untutored children of nature who were little more than a century ago the sole human occupants and proprietors of the vast Northwestern empire, of which Chicago is now the proud metropolis. Pilfered by the advance guard of the whites, oppressed and robbed by government agents, deprived of their lands by the government itself with only scant compensations, shot down by soldiery in wars fomented for the purpose of plundering and destroying their race, and finally drowned by the ever westward tide of population, it is evident there is no future for them except as they may exist as a memory in the sculptor's bronze or stone and the painter's canvas.[72]

At the simple dedication ceremony held June 9, 1894, both Judge Tree's letter and the Park Board's acceptance letter were read. In the acceptance letter, Lincoln Park board president R.A. Waller formally received this second sculpture gift from Judge Tree and added,

There are those still living who may have been eye-witnesses of such a scene as your beautiful gift represents within the very limits of which is now Lincoln Park. The humane and exalted sentiments of your letter. . . inspire the hope that the silent Indian horseman, holding out towards this great city a signal of peace, may be accepted as a public appeal for a more humane and honorable treatment to the few remaining tribes.[73]

Before a crowd of two thousand onlookers, which included Mr. and Mrs. Dallin and Judge Tree, the wife of the artist released the draping American flag from the monument, and the delighted crowd erupted in cheering. With Mr. Dallin having already spoken and Judge Tree refusing to speak, the crowd settled for three rousing cheers to honor the artist and benefactor.

Cyrus Dallin was born and raised on the Utah frontier where interaction with Indians was part of his play. He also played by modeling figures of toys, animals, Indians, and playmates from soft riverbank clay. In 1880, Cyrus moved to Boston to study sculpture, and after two years he set up his own studio. He would take several extended trips to Paris to further his training and development as an artist.

13

John Peter Altgeld

ILLINOIS GOVERNOR

1847–1902

Ask no man! Go out into the night and look straight up to the stars. Take counsel and comfort from them.[74]

John Peter Altgeld

Sunday, June 25, 1893, at Waldheim Cemetery (ninety miles west of Chicago), a crowd of eight thousand assembled for the undraping of a monument honoring five executed Haymarket anarchists. The following day, Illinois Governor John Peter Altgeld pardoned the three still-imprisoned Haymarket convicts. With this act, Governor Altgeld secured his fame while ending his chances for reelection.*

The Haymarket affair of May 4, 1886, began peacefully as a rally in support of striking workers, but ended tragically with a bombing and ensuing police fire. Seven police officers were killed and some sixty policemen were wounded; an unknown number of civilians were injured. The bomber was never identified.†

The Haymarket bombing was a climactic incident in labor's movement for fair pay and decent working conditions. This nationwide movement (part of a larger international cause) largely began after the Civil War and extended for many decades. By the late 1870s, the movement's radical center was Chicago. Siding with workers in Chicago were anarchists and socialists who increasingly called on workers to take up arms and fight. Both sides, business owners and laborers, were guilty of using unnecessary force and thereby escalating violence. In the emotionally elevated aftermath of the Haymarket riot, with the bomber's identity unknown, police resorted to arresting leading radicals. Eight

---

* The back of the Haymarket-Martyrs' Monument names the five anarchists executed November 11, 1887: August Spies, Adolph Fischer, Albert R. Parsons, Louis Lingg, and George Engel (Lingg committed suicide on the eve of his execution). Those pardoned by Altgeld were Michael Schwab, Sam Fielden and Oscar Neebe.

† Police fire after the bombing caused a number of the injuries and contributed to most of the fatalities. One policeman, Officer Mathias J. Degan, died of just bomb wounds.

labor agitators were tried and convicted, and on August 20, 1886, seven were sentenced to death based on their history of inciting violence and, in one case, bomb making. The eighth man received fifteen years imprisonment.

The day before the hanging, November 10, 1887, Governor Richard Oglesby commuted sentences to life imprisonment for the two men who were eligible; they had formally asked for mercy, as the law required.*

The tragedy at Haymarket Square remains controversial even today. Anticipating the controversy of his pardon, Altgeld thoroughly examined the incident's history and trial, and consequently, he wrote an eighteen-thousand-word pardon. In short, Altgeld's pardon asserted: 1) the defendants were not given a fair trial, and 2) they were not proven guilty of the crime charged (i.e. the bombing). Altgeld affirmed, "The State has never discovered who it was that threw the bomb that killed the policeman, and the evidence does not show any connection whatever between the defendants and the man who did throw it."[75]

Before assuming the office of Governor in 1893, Altgeld had a history of siding with society's underdogs. In 1884, he authored *Our Penal Machinery and Its Victims,* a book that critiqued society's harsh treatment of criminals and the poor. He wrote, "The truth is that the great multitudes annually arrested . . . are the poor, the unfortunate, the young and the neglected. . . . In short, our penal machinery seems to recruit its victims from among those that are fighting an unequal fight in the struggle for existence." Altgeld called for a system focused more on curing crime rather than solely punishing. He considered the effect of police brutality in cases of minor crime or merely suspicion:

> Will not those that were already weak and were having a hard struggle for existence, be further weakened, and therefore more liable soon to become actual offenders than they otherwise would have been? . . .
> *Brutal treatment brutalizes* and thus prepares for crime.[76]

Altgeld's family immigrated to Ohio from Germany when he was three months old. At sixteen, Pete—as he was then called—volunteered for four months of Civil War service, where he saw, at most, mild activity. At twenty-two, he left Ohio to make his life out West. To go west, he walked, sleeping most nights under the stars.

---

* Oglesby commuted sentences for Fielden and Schwab.

After some years in St. Louis and Savannah, Missouri, Altgeld finally settled in Chicago, where he worked as a lawyer, a judge, and a real estate developer before serving one term as Illinois Governor, 1893 to 1897.

In 1877 he married Emma Ford, an Ohio girl with whom he fell in love some eight years prior. His disappointment of never becoming a father spurred him all the more to work hard and create lasting contributions.

In siding with the poor and the working class, Altgeld was repeatedly labeled a socialist and an anarchist, but there was nothing socialist or anarchist about his personal story. For the man who had arrived in St. Louis penniless had forged a life of success through hard work, perseverance, and self-reliance. He was a principled public servant who stood staunchly for law and order. At a time when Governor Altgeld was nearing personal bankruptcy, notorious transportation "czar" Charles Yerkes offered Altgeld a small fortune to do nothing: to not veto a bill known as the "eternal monopoly" bills.* Altgeld did veto the bill, and Yerkes, aware of Altgeld's money troubles, was impressed. Of Altgeld, Yerkes remarked, "I admire that man!"[77]

After his governorship, Altgeld remained a vital force in the Democratic Party. Siding with society's underdog to the end, he suffered a stroke moments after delivering a speech protesting Great Britain's war against the Boer Republics. He died early the following morning. Altgeld was just fifty-three.

THE ALTGELD STATUE

ARTIST	Gutzon Borglum (1867–1941)
DATE	September 6, 1915 (Labor Day)
BENEFACTOR	State of Illinois
LOCATION	Just east of Goethe monument
PARTICULARS	Eight-and-a-half-foot-high bronze, staged on a low circular platform

Controversy surrounded the selection of the Altgeld monument just as controversy surrounded the politician. What began as a statue competition with

---

* Had Altgeld accepted Yerkes's bribe and not exercised his veto authority, the "eternal monopoly" bills would have legalized monopoly, allowing Yerkes's the chance of strengthening and lengthening his near-monopoly of Chicago's transit system.

thirty-four entries ended with an awarded commission to a competition non-participant, Gutzon Borglum.*

In September 1913, the Altgeld memorial commission invited artists across the nation to compete for the $25,000 John P. Altgeld statue contract.† Members of the commission, all former friends of Altgeld, were resolved to select an artist who could capture Altgeld's spirit. Louis F. Post, assistant secretary of labor, explained, "We felt ourselves to be true Altgeldians and wanted a truthful portrayal of the spirit of the man himself."[78]

In the first round, after all thirty-four submissions were rejected, five artists were selected to submit modifications. Four of these five finalists were Chicagoans. In the meantime, brother of prominent sculptor Cyrus E. Dallin—creator of *Signal of Peace*—cried foul after Mr. Dallin's entry was denied outright. Cyrus's brother charged that the Altgeld statue commission was fixed.

In the second round, the five modified renditions fared no better. To one critic, only one of the five was not comical, and still this one was not a winner.

Thereafter, the Altgeld statue commission appealed to artists outside the competition, first to a Chicagoan named Haag, and finally to New York artist Gutzon Borglum. The *Chicago Daily Tribune* reported with the headline, "Altgeld Contract Secretly Let to Gotham Sculptor."[79]

Idaho-born Borglum was known worldwide and was considered by some to be the successor to St. Gaudens—sculptor of Lincoln Park's Lincoln monument. Borglum's greatest fame, at that time, was his rendering of Atlas as a woman. Borglum had asserted, "The modern world is held together by adhesion; it is kept together by magnetism, by love. In other words, it is the mother who bears the burden of the world."[80]

Suitably, Lincoln Park's John P. Altgeld memorial was undraped on Labor Day, 1915, before federal and state officials and organized labor. Altgeld's niece, Miss Josephine A. Fredericks, released the covering with a pull of the cord. Governor Edward Dunne formally accepted the statue on behalf of the state. Dunne remembered, "Altgeld was a friend of the common people and never feared to take a stand with them."[81]

---

* Gutzon Borglum, with the assistance of four hundred workers, famously sculpted Mount Rushmore. He would later render Lincoln Park's Sheridan statue, unveiled in 1924.

† Five men comprised the John P. Altgeld memorial commission: Joseph S. Martin; Assistant Secretary of Labor Louis F. Post, State Senator Johann Waage, Daniel L. Cruice, and State Representative Charles A. Karch.

14

Richard J. Oglesby

ILLINOIS GOVERNOR AND UNITED STATES SENATOR

1824–1899

[With respect to rebel soldiers, they] should at last meet face to face the black race of the south . . . and tremble before the men proclaimed by them to have no rights.[82]

Richard J. Oglesby, July 6, 1863[*]

*R*ichard J. Oglesby was thrice popularly elected Illinois governor: 1865 to 1869, 1873 to 1873, and 1885 to 1889. He was once elected U.S. senator by the Illinois legislature, 1873 to 1878. In his final term as governor, Oglesby became known worldwide for his role in the Haymarket affair.[†]

Governor Oglesby was the last in line to pass judgment on convicted Chicago Haymarket anarchists. After a jury of twelve sentenced seven anarchists to death, the Illinois Supreme Court upheld the appealed case, and the United States Supreme Court refused to hear it. Consequently, seven men awaited execution by hanging on November 11, 1887. On the eve of the executions, Oglesby commuted sentences to life in prison for the two anarchists who formally had petitioned for mercy, as the law required for commutation. Oglesby's written statement explained, "A most careful consideration of the whole subject leads me to the conclusion that the sentence of the law as to Samuel Fielden and Michael Schwab, may be modified . . . in the interest of humanity and without doing violence to public justice." He closed, "While I would gladly have come to a different conclusion in regard to the sentences of defendants, August Spies, Adolph Fisher [sic] George Engel, Albert R. Parsons and Louis Lingg, I regret to

---

[*] After sustaining a major injury in the Civil War battle at Corinth, Richard Oglesby wrote these words as part of a final order to his men. Around that time, the Union Army had begun recruiting blacks into service, a policy that Oglesby supported.

[†] The Haymarket affair of Tuesday, May 4, 1886, left seven police officers dead, sixty wounded, and injured an unknown number of civilians, assumed to be about equal in number to what the police suffered. Chicago German-American anarchists who were rallying in support of striking workers led the terror, which began with a bomb.

say that under the solemn sense of obligations of my office, I have been unable to do so."[83]

Oglesby's popularity with the people of Illinois grew out of respect for his military service, his talents as a prolific Republican-Party stump speaker, and from his political and personal association with Abraham Lincoln.

As did so many Illinois men, Oglesby served admirably in the Civil War, where he achieved the rank of brigadier general before suffering a near fatal injury in October 1862.[*] He was shot below his left armpit, above his heart, and the rebel bullet would remain lodged in his chest for the remainder of his days.

Oglesby was a sought-after political stump speaker for the Illinois Republican Party. In entertaining speeches, which continued for hours, Oglesby promoted candidates and causes close to his heart: abolition of slavery, pro-war patriotism, veteran advocacy, and African American suffrage.

Oglesby and Lincoln became political allies and friends in the early days of the Illinois Republican Party.[†] Oglesby played a supportive role in Lincoln's political career, travelling throughout Illinois to speak on Lincoln's behalf—before and after Lincoln's election to the nation's highest office. And when, by chance, Oglesby was able to be at Lincoln's deathbed, Oglesby, from that earliest moment, assumed much of the responsibility for carrying on Lincoln's memory.

Like Lincoln, Oglesby was born in Kentucky. Orphaned at eight, the meagerly schooled boy grew to enjoy a remarkably active and honorable life. At twenty-two, Oglesby volunteered for an adventurous year of service in the Mexican War. In 1851, upon returning (modestly) enriched from the California Gold Rush of 1849, he kept a boyhood promise and freed a former-family slave, sixty-five-year-old Uncle Tim (Tilman). And apparently needing a break from his law practice and promising political career, thirty-two-year-old Oglesby took a twenty-month grand tour of Europe, a trip highlighted with excursions to the Holy Land and to Czar Alexander II of Russia's coronation in Moscow.

Oglesby's first wife, Anna Elizabeth White Oglesby, died at thirty-four of tuberculosis, while Oglesby was serving his first term as governor. She left the governor with two surviving children of four born. Five years later he married Emma Gillett Keays, with whom he would have four more children. Matrimony

---

[*] The American Civil War was waged from April 12, 1861, to April 9, 1865.
[†] The Illinois Republican Party formed to oppose the extension of slavery.

agreed with the governor. On their fourth anniversary, he wrote Emma's mother thanking her for "the precious gift of your lovely daughter."[84]

At seventy-five, weakened by influenza, the former governor fell in his home and died of a concussion to the brain.

On the day of his funeral in Elkhart, Illinois, Oglesby was honored with an elaborate procession of military men and town bands. Thousands of admirers arrived by train to attend the service. But most special of all was the presence of the flag that had draped Lincoln's coffin; for the first time, it was removed from the state museum. And after apparently being carried in the funeral procession, this piece of history graced Oglesby's casket at the burial service, linking him once more to the martyred president, in death as he had been in life.[*]

OGLESBY STATUE

ARTIST	Leonard Crunelle (1872–1944)
DATE	November 21, 1919
BENEFACTOR	John Payne, J.S. Runnels, John Bunn, L.C. LaForce, and Martin Bailey
LOCATION	On a knoll between North Pond and the Hamilton statue
PARTICULARS	Ten-foot-high bronze

In 1885, while Oglesby served his final term as governor, his likeness was one of eight portrait statues planned for placement high in the dome of the new state capitol building.[†] This honor was never realized, however. Oglesby denied himself the distinction sometime between March 16 and August 17, 1887. He apparently did not want the distraction at a time of pronounced social unrest: strikes were commonplace, and the result of the Haymarket case's appeal was looming.

---

[*] Oglesby's funeral and burial were held on separate days, April 28 and May 8, 1899, as the arrival of family was awaited.

[†] The remaining celebrated figures included Ninian Edwards, territorial governor and third governor of Illinois; Shadrach Bond, the state's first governor; Sidney Breese, state supreme court justice; Ulysses S. Grant, president; Lyman Trumbull, U.S. senator; John A. Logan, U.S. senator; and William Morrison, U.S. congressman. The likeness of former governor Edward Coles would replace Oglesby's likeness.

Years later, friends and supporters of Oglesby's legacy reinitiated the raising of his likeness, this time on a knoll that modestly rises just north of North Pond in Lincoln Park.

At a dedication ceremony held November 21, 1919, before two hundred supporters, Governor Oglesby's life and memory was celebrated. Family members present were the former governor's widow; his son, Lieutenant Governor John G. Oglesby; daughter Miss Felicite Oglesby; and probably grandson Richard J. Oglesby III. (The *Chicago Daily Tribune* alternatively reported a Richard J. Oglesby II as present, but no family member was so named.) In heavy rain, Governor Frank O. Lowden accepted the statue and said in part, "I think I may say without detraction that no man in all our history was ever as close to the hearts of the people of Illinois as Richard J. Oglesby. His career recounted in simple words upon the bronze plate beyond the statue reads like a romance."[85]

15

Eugene Field

CHILDREN'S POET

1850–1895

Wynken and Blynken are two little eyes,
  And Nod is a little head,
And the wooden shoe that sailed the skies
  Is a wee one's trundle-bed.
So shut your eyes while mother sings
  Of wonderful sights that be,
And you shall see the beautiful things
  As you rock in the misty sea,
  Where the old shoe rocked the fishermen three:
    Wynken,
    Blynken,
    And Nod.

(Eugene Field, "Wynken, Blynken
and Nod," fourth and final stanza)

"[Field] wrote so that a grown-up—be he ever so old and ever so far removed from the mystery of the child world—could see and understand and find in his heart once more the fleeting days of his childhood."—*Kansas City Star*[86]

*I*n 1883, famed journalist Eugene Field was lured to Chicago from Denver and began writing his humorous "Sharps and Flats" column for the Chicago *Daily Record*. While Field wrote in a variety of genres, he was best loved as the "Poet of Childhood." His most recited verses include "Wynken, Blynken and Nod," "The Sugar-Plum Tree," and "Little Boy Blue."

"Little Boy Blue," the most celebrated poem during Field's lifetime, captures the spirit of a little boy who, after talking with his toy dog and soldier at

bedtime, is visited by an angel in his sleep and presumably never awakens.* Boy Blue scolded,

> "Now, don't you go till I come," he said
> "And don't you make any noise!"
> So toddling off to his trundle-bed
> He dreamed of the pretty toys.

Faithfully, Little Boy Blue's toys remained true and stood in place:

> And they wonder, as waiting these long years through,
> In the dust of that little chair,
> What has become of our Little Boy Blue
> Since he kissed them and put them there.

Field's tender view of childhood can perhaps be linked to the early loss of his mother, brothers, and sisters. His mother died when he was six, and six of seven siblings did not survive infancy. His own family endured similar tragedy—three of his eight children did not reach adulthood.

THE EUGENE FIELD MEMORIAL

ARTIST	Edward McCartan (1879–1947)
DATE	October 9, 1922
BENEFACTOR	Friends, colleagues, the general public, and the Ferguson Fund
LOCATION	Within confines of Lincoln Park Zoo, near the lion house†
PARTICULARS	Eleven-foot-high bronze, atop pink granite base

Shortly after Eugene Field passed away in 1895, Chicago newspapers formed a committee to raise funds for a Eugene Field memorial. Nothing came of this

---

* In 1944, a Chicago lawyer and poet, Charles Newton French, claimed to have authored the original version, "Boy Blue," which he apparently submitted to the *Chicago Daily News* in 1884. Based on evidence French provided, the author of *Field Days: The Life, Times & Reputation of Eugene Field* believes it reasonable to assume that Field adapted and recast the verse published in 1888.

† Originally "Dream Lady" stood at the entrance to the small animal house. Its location interfered with building traffic, however, so in early 1948, it was moved to its current site north of the building.

effort, but eighteen years later, a second group organized for the same purpose. Charles G. Dawes, president of the Central Trust of Illinois, spearheaded the effort to raise $10,000. Donors included friends and associates of Field, the general public, and the Ferguson Fund.*

Twenty-seven years after his death, Eugene Field was finally memorialized in Lincoln Park with a monument commonly referred to as "Dream Lady." Field's grandchildren—Jean Field Foster, six, and Robert Eugene Field, two years old—together tugged the cord to undrape the bronze. Not technically a portrait statue, the form depicts the female angel from Field's poem "The Rock-a-By Lady" dropping flowers of poetry over two slumbering children at her feet.

The rectangular stone base features child-high relief panels illustrating four of Field's poems: "Wynken, Blynken and Nod," "The Sugar-Plum Tree," "Seein' Things," and "The Fly Away Horse." Two of these are situated on the base's sides, above child-high drinking fountains.

Additionally, excerpts from "Wynken, Blynken, and Nod" and "The Sugar-Plum Tree" are inscribed into the granite. They read:

Wynken, Blynken, and Nod one night
Sailed off in a wooden shoe--
Sailed on a river of crystal light,
Into a sea of dew

Have you ever heard of the Sugar-Plum Tree?
'T is a marvel of great renown!
It blooms on the shore of the Lollipop sea
In the garden of Shut-Eye Town

Melville E. Stone, former head of the Associated Press, spoke in tribute to Field. Stone remembered, "He was a many-sided character. He had a profoundly religious, even spiritual, nature. The Puritan strain of his ancestry frequently cropped out in his daily life. Yet over all there spread the warm, mellow rays of human sympathy that prompted his verse. He sounded all depths of tender emotion and voiced the agonized cry of bereaved motherhood, sisterhood, childhood, with the tone and tempo of a master."[87]

* In 1905, pioneer lumber merchant Benjamin Franklin Ferguson gave $1,000,000 to Chicago for the erection of statuary "commemorating worthy men and women of America or important events of American history." Income from the Ferguson Fund perpetual trust would fund sculpture at the discretion of Art Institute trustees. (*Chicago Daily Tribune,* "Gives $1,000,000 for Chicago Art," Apr. 15, 1905)

16

Greene Vardiman Black

NORTHWESTERN UNIVERSITY DENTAL SCHOOL DEAN

1836–1915

> The day is surely coming, and perhaps within the lifetime of you young
> men before me, when we will be engaged in practicing preventive, rather
> than reparative, dentistry.[88]
>
> Greene Vardiman Black, 1896 statement to dental students

The year Greene Vardiman Black was born, one of the leading dentists at the time warned:

> One thing is certain, this profession must either rise or sink. If means are not taken
> to suppress and discountenance the malpractices of the multitude of incompetent
> persons, who are pressing into it, merely for the sake of its emoluments, it must
> sink;—for the few competent and well-educated men, who are now upholding it,
> will abandon a disreputable profession . . . and turn their attention to some other
> calling more congenial to the feelings of honorable and enlightened men.[89, *]

In the early 1800s, while there were some trained and skilled dental specialists, most patients relied on self-taught dental practitioners. Dental instruction was published in periodicals such as *The Family Physician and Guide to Health* (published in upstate New York), which in 1833 directed, "Any person attending to the following directions will be as well qualified to extract teeth as the best surgeon in the Union." The text continued, "the teeth may be turned [with a key] either out or in, but it will be found most convenient to turn the double teeth in and the single, or forward, teeth out."[90, †] Such words cause the modern reader to cringe, especially in light of the fact that anesthesia was not introduced until 1844.

---

* Shearjashub Spoon wrote the above quote in his *Guide to Sound Teeth, or, A Popular Treatise on the Teeth* (1836).

† The early-American tooth extraction instrument looked like a large key and so was referred to as such.

Green Vardiman Black was a leader in progressing the field of dentistry. As professor of pathology and bacteriology, starting in 1891, and later as dean of the newly organized Northwestern University Dental School, Black advanced dentistry through his research, published writings, and teachings. He is often referred to as the father of scientific dentistry or the father of modern dentistry.

BLACK STATUE

ARTIST   Frederick Hibbard (1881–1950)

DATE   August 8, 1918

BENEFACTOR   National Dental Association

LOCATION   Intersection of North Avenue and Astor Street*

PARTICULARS   Six-and-a half-foot-high bronze

The National Dental Association convened in Chicago for its annual meeting in August 1918. After more than seventeen hundred dental professionals lunched in the Auditorium Hotel on August 8, an afternoon unveiling ceremony was held in Lincoln Park for the Greene Vardiman Black memorial.

Dr. Frank O. Hedrick of Ottawa, Kansas, former president of the association, spoke in tribute to Dr. Black.

An inscription on the statue's base reads, "Father of modern dentistry, born on the prairies of central Illinois, self-educated, he became in his profession the foremost scientific investigator, writer and teacher of his time."

---

* For thirty-one years the Black statue stood at its original location, the northeast corner of Clark Street and North Avenue. In or around January 1950, it was moved to its present location, so that the Chicago Transit Authority could build a bus turnaround lane.

Missing Portrait Statues

GARIBALDI STATUE

RELOCATED	1982
HONORING	Giuseppe Garibaldi Italian general and republican reformer 1807–1882
ARTIST	Victor Gherardi of New York City
DATE	October 12, 1901
BENEFACTOR	Legione Garibaldi
LOCATION	The empty pedestal still stands just south of South Pond.
PARTICULARS	Bronze, an estimated nine-and-a-half-feet high, originally stood in Lincoln Park upon a sixteen-foot-high granite rock

The Garibaldi statue has graced four separate locations in Chicago. In 1901, the monument was installed at the southeast corner of present-day Fullerton Avenue and Cannon Drive. By 1919, newspaper accounts situate the Garibaldi monument just east of Clark Street, near the Wisconsin Street intersection. In 1934, the bronze, with its massive base, was relocated further east to just south of South Pond, where its pedestal remains today. The Garibaldi Society of Chicago had petitioned the Lincoln Park commissioners for this new location; they were seeking a friendlier site for their annual Garibaldi birthday celebration. The final and current statue home was made in 1982, to adorn the newly named Garibaldi Park.

Giuseppe Garibaldi was an Italian patriot and revolutionary who fought for the freedom and unification of Italy. His fame as a guerrilla warfare technician prompted President Lincoln to offer him rank in the American Civil War, an honor that Garibaldi refused.

In celebrating the hero of a united Italy, some two thousand Italian sympathizers paraded in steady rain from City Hall north to Fullerton Parkway for the statue unveiling ceremony held October 12, 1901.

CAPTAIN MAGNUS ANDERSEN BUST

REMOVED	1995
HONORING	Captain Magnus Andersen Adventurist 1857–1938
ARTIST	Carl Paulsen
DATE	September 13, 1936
BENEFACTOR	Norwegian League
LOCATION	At one time, northeast of Armitage Avenue, within zoo confines near the duck pond
PARTICULARS	Bronze, estimated to be between two and three feet high, once mounted on a stone pedestal.

While the World's Columbian Exposition of 1893 commemorated Christopher Columbus's coming to America in 1492, Norway's Captain Magnus Andersen used the occasion to celebrate Lief Ericson's new world arrival some five hundred years earlier.

In 1880, along the southern coast of Norway, an ancient Viking ship was discovered. At the time, it was estimated to be between eight hundred and one thousand years old, therefore overlapping the date of Ericson's legendary landing in America. Inspired, Andersen thought to build a replica of the ancient vessel and sail it to Chicago's World's Fair.

After safely crossing the Atlantic in May, the Viking ship, ornamented with a dragonhead and tail, arrived in Chicago on July 12, 1893, via the Erie Canal and the Great Lakes. Before more than one hundred thousand onlookers, it sailed past Lincoln Park for an afternoon arrival in Jackson Park. Thereafter the dragon ship was a major attraction at the Fair and was seen by hundreds of thousands of fairgoers. Worldwide, newspapers reported Andersen's dramatic feat. Finally, the capability of Viking ship engineering had been proved.

In 1933, Andersen relived his spirited voyage to arrive at Chicago's Century of Progress exposition, this time in a modern vessel.

For roughly seventy-five years, Andersen's Viking ship rested in Lincoln Park, until it was removed in 1995. In 1936, the Norwegian League of Chicago adorned the Viking ship exhibit with the Captain Magnus Andersen bust, to commemorate his two historic voyages.*

BEETHOVEN BUST

STOLEN	April 1971
HONORING	Ludwig von Beethoven German musician 1770–1827
ARTIST	Johannes Gelert (1852–1923)
DATE	June 19, 1897
BENEFACTOR	Carl Wolfsohn (1834–1907)
LOCATION	Once stood in Grandmother's Garden, across Stockton Drive from and slightly north of the Schiller statue (Webster Avenue). A remnant of the base remains.
PARTICULARS	Bronze, three feet in height, atop a five-foot pedestal

Once facing the Friedrich von Schiller statue, the Beethoven bust had inscribed on its pedestal, "Alle menschen werden brueder," *All men are brothers*. These words taken from Schiller's poem "Ode to Joy," inspired Beethoven's final complete symphony, his Symphony No. 9.

Stolen in 1971, the three-foot bust stood atop a five-foot pedestal of beveled raindrop stone. Gelert, sculptor of Lincoln Park's Hans Christian Andersen

---

* The Viking ship and Andersen monument are presently in storage, awaiting some permanent exhibit. The ship's dragon "head" and "tail" are in storage at the Museum of Science and Industry. The Viking ship, currently in Geneva, Illinois, is in desperate need of restoration funding.

likeness, had depicted the composer gazing upward. The benefactor, German-born Carl Wolfsohn, was a teacher, pianist, conductor, and musical scholar, and he gave the $3,000 bronze to celebrate his fifty years as a musician.

Held on a cloudless day, June 19, 1897, the undraping ceremony included a performance of Beethoven's music by the sixty-voice German Maennerchor. Carl Wolfsohn spoke to the crowd of music lovers, including the Beethoven Society, which he helped found. He said,

> My heart is full of gratitude that fate has enabled me to give the city of my adoption and its people this gift. Beethoven's genius has been the safeguard in my long musical career . . . I have felt it a thousand times what Beethoven said of his own music. . . , "I fear not the fate of my music; it cannot fare ill. He who comprehends it will be free of all woe which burdens others."

In closing Mr. Wolfsohn said,

> Beethoven and Schiller face each other, both having possessed those divine sparks of genius that give them immortality. And when the hundreds and thousands that seek rest and recreation in our park pass this beautiful spot, standing before this monument, ask who is this, let the answer be given: "Ludwig von Beethoven, the greatest musician and greatest benefactor of mankind."[91]

SOLTI BUST

RELOCATED	October 2006
HONORING	Sir Georg Solti Chicago Symphony Orchestra music director 1912–1997
ARTIST	Elizabeth Frink (1930–1993)
DATE	October 1987
BENEFACTOR	Geraldine Freund (1910–2005)
LOCATION	Once stood in formal gardens near the Lincoln Park Conservatory
PARTICULARS	Bronze, three feet in height, atop a six-foot black granite pedestal

Art patron Geraldine Freund presented the $20,000 Solti bust to maestro Georg Solti on his seventy-fifth birthday, October 21, 1987. The bronze was the work of London's Elizabeth Frink, and it was set in Lincoln Park's formal gardens, near the Lincoln Park Conservatory.

Freund was reportedly disappointed with its limestone base; she had envisioned a marble pedestal instead. Park district representatives, however, insisted that the $25,000 support would not be replaced.*

In October 2006, nineteen years after its unveiling, the Solti likeness was moved to Grant Park's newly created Sir Georg Solti Garden, near Symphony Center. Now mounted on dark granite, it respectfully faces the Spirit of Music statue, which honors Theodore Thomas, founding conductor of the Chicago Symphony Orchestra.

Hungarian-born Georg Solti famously served as conductor of the Chicago Symphony Orchestra for twenty-two years.

LINNÉ STATUE

RELOCATED	March 1976
HONORING	Carl von Linné Swedish botanist 1707–1778
ARTIST	Original statue in Stockholm, Sweden, by Frithiof Kjellberg (1836–1885); Chicago replica created by Carl Johan Dyfverman (1844–1892)
DATE	May 23, 1891
BENEFACTOR	Swedes of Chicago
LOCATION	Once located on the southeast corner of Fullerton Avenue and Stockton Drive. The statue stood very close to the curb after Fullerton Avenue was extended to Lakeshore Drive, approximately fifty years after the monument was first erected.

---

* The original limestone base was in fact a "recycled" pedestal, one that originally propped the *Charitas* statue that once graced Simmons Island in Lincoln Park. See the Epilogue for more information on the *Charitas* statue.

Bronze, fifteen feet in height; including its massive (Vermont) granite pedestal and base, the figure reached a height of thirty-nine feet. Four female figures, made of zinc and iron, decorated the base. These muses, each six feet high, were symbolic of the sciences in which Linné was distinguished: botany, medicine, mineralogy, and zoology.

Botany held a flower and magnifying lens. Medicine grasped a mortar and pestle whilst a snake crossed her thigh. Mineralogy studied a prism-shaped rock. And zoology was bedecked with a crane-like bird and a butterfly.

After having been repeatedly damaged by vandals, the figures were removed. One damaged muse is exhibited at the Swedish American Museum. The remaining three muses are either in storage or lost.*

In March of 1976, without warning, park district workmen dismantled the Carl von Linné statue at Fullerton Avenue and Stockton Drive. Dismayed onlookers snapped photos, contacted Friends of the Park, and, in one case reportedly, wept. Within days, a genuine brouhaha was brewing, as locals, including the alderman, demanded a replacement statue.

Unbeknownst to the wider public, Chicago Swedish Americans had been lobbying for fifty years to relocate the Linné bronze. The reason: a friendlier location for their annual outdoor celebration.† An invitation from University of Chicago's Nobel prize-winning biologist and president emeritus, George W. Beadle, coupled with a nod of approval from Mayor Daley, and the deal was finally done, paid for by Chicago Swedes.

By April 19, 1976, Linne's likeness had a new home on the Midway Plaisance at the University of Chicago, in time for King Carl XVI Gustaf of Sweden's Chicago visit.

---

* At the statue's 1891 erection, the muses were not yet in place. The original intent was to cast bronze muses from the zinc and iron models, which had been shipped from Sweden for casting purposes. (These figures had been used in casting the Linné statue in Stockholm, Sweden.) With time, interest was lost and money was lacking; and so alternatively, the casting figures were mounted in March 1893. Unfortunately the metal of the casting muses was subject to deterioration and consequently vandalism.

† The widening and extension of Fullerton Avenue, as part of Lake Shore Drive improvements, had left the statue dangerously close to traffic.

Prior to relocating the monument, research had revealed the existence of a time capsule from its 1891 erection. Opening the eighty-five-year-old treasure box revealed Chicago Swedish newspapers, books about Linné, Swedish coins dating to 1735, pressed Linné flowers native to Sweden, and more—thirty-eight pieces of memorabilia in all. After adding new remembrances from the king's visit, the time capsule was reburied in the statue.

Carl von Linné was the first to scientifically classify the kingdom of plants. His Chicago likeness is copied from an original that stands in Stockholm, Sweden.

THE SPIRIT OF THE AMERICAN DOUGHBOY

REMOVED   Probably 1946

HONORING   Men and women who served in World War I

ARTIST   E.M. Viquesney (1876–1946)

DATE   November 11, 1927

BENEFACTOR   Kiwanis Clubs of Chicago*

LOCATION   Just east of where Briar Place meets the park

PARTICULARS   Life-sized form of hollow pressed copper

For nineteen years, men and women who served in World War I were honored in Lincoln Park with an American Doughboy statue. The memorial depicted an infantryman in "No Man's Land," advancing in a terrain with barbed-wire entanglements. In one hand the figure held a rifle, in the other hand, a grenade held high. Engraved on a plaque were the words: "In grateful recognition of the patriotic service rendered by the men and women of Chicago during the World War, 1914–1918. Kiwanis Clubs of Chicago."

More than five thousand R.O.T.C. cadets, military units, club members, and public officials celebrated the undraping on Armistice Day, November 11, 1927, and on each following Armistice Day, the Kiwanis clubs placed a wreath at the base of the statue.

---

* Kiwanis clubs were founded in 1915, originally as joint business and service organizations.

In 1946, the poorly made hollow sculpture was irreparably vandalized. Soon thereafter, the injured form was permanently removed. Ernest Moore Viquensey claimed that more than three hundred of his American Doughboy statues were erected throughout the United States. The most prominent one today stands in Chicago. Originally unveiled in 1926 in Garfield Park, it too was vandalized, sometime in the 1960s. In 2003, after decades in storage, the nearly forgotten relic was beautifully restored to permanently honor Soldier Field.

SWEDENBORG BUST

STOLEN	Mid-January 1976
HONORING	Emanuel Swedenborg Scientist, philosopher, and mystic 1688–1772
ARTIST	Adolf Jonsson (Swedish)
DATE	June 28, 1924
BENEFACTOR	Bust contributed by Mr. and Mrs. L. Brackett Bishop, with pedestal contributed by Swedes of Chicago
LOCATION	East of Lake Shore Drive between Fullerton and Diversey
PARTICULARS	Bronze, three feet, eight inches in height

In a world in which the voice of conscience too often seems still and small there is need of that spiritual leadership of which Swedenborg was a particular example.
        Franklin D. Roosevelt, 1938
        (pedestal inscription)

Thirty-four years after its disappearance, the Chicago Park District still hopes to install a duplicate Emanuel Swedenborg bust to its wanting base and steps, which are situated east of Lakeshore Drive, between Fullerton and Diversey. The restoration became a repair project, as well, after a drunken driver ploughed into and damaged the structure in late October 2009. Using archived photos, the monument can be replicated as soon as funds are made available.

The Swedenborg bronze mysteriously disappeared mid-January 1976. At the time, police speculated that thieves were not interested in the artwork, but rather in the mass of metal, valued at $10,000.

Mr. and Mrs. Brackett Bishop of Chicago commissioned the $1,000 Lincoln Park original bust and presented it in 1924. Their commission was a reproduction of an earlier likeness fashioned in 1919 by artist Adolf Jonsson of Stockholm.

Chicago Swedish newspapers, at the time, recorded the only known reports of the 1924 bust undraping. Translations made the following year provide English accounts of the June 24, 1924 celebration.

Early in the festivities, a Professor C. G. Wallenius addressed the crowd of some ten thousand Chicago Swedes, including a throng of white-capped singers and a nearby floating Viking ship bedecked with maidens. Professor Wallenius began,

> Here we stand before the image of a man whose genius was so colossal and all embracing that a right conception of him presents some difficulties. His lifework may be divided into two periods. During the first period, he chiefly presents himself as a great investigator and scientist, and during a later period of life he presents the picture of a supernatural prophet and seer.

The professor continued,

> A change took place in his mode of thinking . . . when he reached the age of fifty-seven years. . . . From a great scientist, he became an equally great religious thinker, philosopher and seer. Religion, in its period of enlightenment, did not reach a higher plane than he. . . . He had made himself the spokesmen of a mystically religious and speculative doctrine, in which he claimed positive revelations from God Himself, from the angels, and from the spiritual world, hidden beyond the earthly sphere of mankind.

Near the closing of his speech, Professor Wallenius summarized,

> The quintessence of his teaching is found in his conception of God. He rediscovered the old principle of John, that God, in His inmost essence, is Love, and that He reveals Himself in Wisdom and intelligence. . . .[92]

After a letter of greeting from President Calvin Coolidge was read, the benefactor, Mr. Bishop, recited a poem on Swedenborg by author Edwin Markham. The final orator was Swedish minister to the United States, Mr. Axel Wallenberg, who concluded his presentation with the words:

We acknowledge that Swedenborg was great as a scientist, but still greater as our religious teacher, and we are proud to see his memory honored as such a teacher. But we are still prouder to see the great Swede installed among the memorialized of a great nation, a nation which knows of no boundaries when it comes to cultural and scientific developments, and which has accepted the theory that what is best on the globe shall become the characteristics of the American people.[93]

Lastly, a young girl tugged ropes to remove the Swedish and American flag draping. Festivities concluded with the singing of "America."

Postscript

Briefly detailed below are sculptures that *do not* satisfy the portrait statue or vintage statue parameters, but which decorate or have decorated Lincoln Park.

Other Sculptures

Bates Fountain (also known as *Storks at Play*)

ARTIST   Augustus Saint-Gaudens and Frederick MacMonnies

DATE   1887

BENEFACTOR   Eli Bates

LOCATION   Just north of the Schiller statue

PARTICULARS   The fountain includes six bronze figures; three mermen handling large fish and three large birds (originally identified as herons), at play in a pool, around a centerpiece of cattails.

Curve XXII (I Will)

ARTIST   Ellsworth Kelly

DATE   1981

BENEFACTOR   Conceived of by Friends of the Park and paid for by contributions from more than two thousand individuals, a City of Chicago grant, and a National Endowment for the Arts grant.

LOCATION   Northeast corner of Fullerton Avenue and Cannon Drive

PARTICULARS   Nicknamed *I Will*, it celebrates the can-do spirit Chicagoans exhibited in rebuilding the city from ashes. Its shape suggests the modern skyscrapers that Chicago "gave birth to" after the fire.

Totem Pole of Kwanusila, the Thunderbird

ARTIST   Tony Hunt of Fort Rupert, British Columbia (a descendent of the original pole's carver, George Hunt)

DATE   March 21, 1986

BENEFACTOR   Kraft, Incorporated

LOCATION   In the park at Addison Street

PARTICULARS   The carving is an authentic totem pole of the Kwakiutl First Nations tribe. The base is the head of a sea monster. The shaft is a whale ridden by the human figure on its back, and perched on top is Kwanusila, the Thunderbird.

Carved into red cedar wood, this forty-foot-tall totem pole is an exact replica of the original one on this site dedicated June 20, 1929 and gifted by the founder of Kraft, James L. Kraft. Both dedications were made to the schoolchildren of Chicago. The first carving was returned to British Columbia for study and conservation. After years of wear and maintenance, it had lost much of its original design.

Dr. Jose Rizal
Philippine Nationalist
1861–1896

ARTIST   Antonio T. Mondejar

DATE   June 19, 1999

BENEFACTOR   Project began by the Malaya Chapter of the Order of the Knights of Rizal and the Ladies for Rizal. Funds collected with the help of Chicagoans of Filipino heritage.

LOCATION   West of N. Lake Shore Drive, just north of Wilson Avenue

PARTICULARS   Rizal is a national hero to the Philippine nation. Highly educated, he was a man of many talents. During the Spanish colonial period, Rizal advocated national liberation, a cause that led to his execution on December 30, 1896. Rizal scholars believe that his death helped fuel the Philippine Revolution.

Missing Sculptures

Fountain Girl*

ARTIST   George E. Wade (London, England)

DATE   June 24, 1921 (its second installation)

BENEFACTOR   Loyal Temperance Legion of Boys and Girls of the World

LOCATION   At the time of its disappearance, the bronze sat atop a horse-drinking trough situated south of an equestrian underpass at present-day West LaSalle Drive, east of the Chicago History Museum.

PARTICULARS   One-cent donations from boys and girls from fifty-seven countries defrayed the statue's cost. *Fountain Girl* was originally unveiled April 17, 1895, at the site of the Women's Temperance Union Temple on the corner of LaSalle and Monroe Streets. It decorated the horse-drinking trough at this downtown intersection. See photos at www.lincolnparkstatues.com.

Mysteriously the three-hundred-pound form disappeared March 1, 1958. *Fountain Girl* is scheduled to be reinstalled in 2011.

Charitas

ARTIST   Ida McClelland Stout

DATE   1922

BENEFACTOR   The *Chicago Daily News*

LOCATION   *Charitas* once graced Simmons Island, parkland east of Lakeshore Drive between Fullerton Avenue and Diversey Parkway that is no longer an island. (A plaque-decorated boulder on Simmons Island details that in 1920, this man-made picnic island was named to honor Francis T. Simmons, a former Lincoln Park Commissioner.) The bronze was situated west of the *Chicago Daily News*'s Fresh Air Sanitarium, a center of caring for Chicago's underprivileged children. The Fresh Air Sanitarium is today the Theatre in the Park.

---

* As *Giants in the Park* goes to print, *Fountain Girl* is still missing, however a newly recast form awaits reinstallation.

In 1940, *Charitas* was removed to allow the construction of a ramp from Fullerton Avenue to Lakeshore Drive. Currently in storage, *Charitas* for a time adorned the Palm House at Garfield Park's Conservatory (installed in the 1980s and removed in the early 2000s).

PARTICULARS "Charitas" or "Love" depicted a mother holding two babes. It was the result of a design competition sponsored by the *Chicago Daily News,* and it symbolized charitable assistance to the city's disadvantaged youth.

While at Garfield Park, the form was painted white, presumably to match the Conservatory's Lorado Taft marble sculptures, *Pastoral* and *Idyl.* The park district's conservator has since removed the paint and restored the bronze. Park district historians are prepared to reinstall *Charitas* in Lincoln Park, should funds be made available. It would be returned with its original pedestal, which for a time supported the Solti bust in Lincoln Park.

Endnotes

INTRODUCTION

1   "Hidden Truths," Bannos, http://hiddentruths.northwestern.edu/confusion/numbers. html.

2   "Hidden Truths," Bannos, http://hiddentruths.northwestern.edu/lincoln_park/early_ years.html.

3   Ibid.

4   "Hidden Truths," Bannos, http://hiddentruths.northwestern.edu/confusion/numbers. html.

5   "Hidden Truths," Bannos, http://hiddentruths.northwestern.edu/couch/why_left.html.

6   "Lincoln Park: Working Out the Assessment," *Chicago Daily Tribune*, February 18, 1877.

7   Miller, *City of the Century*, 170.

8   "Cost of the 'White," *Chicago Daily Tribune*, November 12, 1893.

ABRAHAM LINCOLN

9   Donald, *Lincoln*, 514.

10   Ibid., 223.

11   Ibid., 462.

12   "Abraham Lincoln: Second Inaugural Address," copyright 2010 Bartleby.com, http:// www.bartleby.com/124/pres32.html; Donald, *Lincoln*, 566–567.

13   Donald, *Lincoln*, 592.

14   "Eli Bates' Great Gift," *Chicago Daily Tribune*, October 20, 1887.

15   Taft, *Modern Tendencies in Sculpture*, 106.

16   "The Martyr President," *Chicago Daily Tribune*, October 23, 1887.

RENE-ROBERT DE LA SALLE

17   Johnson, *La Salle*, 112.

18   Ibid., 104.

19   "De La Salle in Bronze," *Chicago Daily Tribune*, October 12, 1889.

20   "Lincoln Park Enriched," *Chicago Daily Tribune*, October 13, 1889.

21   Ibid.

BENJAMIN FRANKLIN

22   Isaacson, *Benjamin Franklin*, 339.

23   Ibid., 145.

24   Ibid., 3.

25   Ibid., 98.

26 Ibid., 140.

27 Ibid., 289.

28 Ibid., 144.

29 "Ben Franklin in Bronze," *Chicago Daily Tribune,* October 17, 1885.

30 "Benjamin Franklin, Printer, Inventor, Philosopher, Educator, Diplomatist, and Statesman," *Chicago Daily Tribune,* June 7, 1896.

ULYSSES S. GRANT

31 Ballard, *U.S. Grant,* 3.

32 Perret, *Ulysses S. Grant,* 286.

33 Ibid., 313–314.

34 Ibid., 312.

35 Ibid., 365.

36 Ibid., 262.

37 Ibid., 292.

38 "The Unveiling of the Grant Statue," *Chicago Daily Tribune,* October 8, 1891.

39 "Acceptance of the Memorial," *Chicago Daily Tribune,* October 8, 1891.

40 Benjamin Harrison, "Judge W.Q. Gresham's Oration," *Chicago Daily Tribune,* October 8, 1891.

HANS CHRISTIAN ANDERSEN

41 Tatar, *Annotated Hans Christian Andersen,* 13.

42 "Children Pay For It," *Chicago Daily Tribune,* February 3, 1893.

FRIEDRICH VON SCHILLER

43 "Gazed on by Thousands: The Schiller Monument Unveiled Amid Great Enthusiasm," *Chicago Daily Tribune,* May 16, 1886.

44 Ibid.

45 Ibid.

46 Ibid.

47 "Poet Schiller is Extolled," *Chicago Daily Tribune,* November 11, 1909.

WILLIAM SHAKESPEARE

48 Greenblatt, *Will in the World,* 17.

49 Ibid., 145.

50 Ibid, 18.

51 "Shakespeare as in Life," *Chicago Daily Tribune,* February 11, 1890.

52 "Unveil the Statue," *Chicago Daily Tribune,* April 24, 1894.

ALEXANDER HAMILTON

53 "Alexander Hamilton, Report on Public Credit, 9 Jan. 1790," The Founders' Constitution, copyright 1987 by The University of Chicago, a joint venture of the University of Chicago Press and the Liberty Fund, http://press-pubs.uchicago.edu/founders/documents/a1_8_2s5.html.

54 Chernow, *Alexander Hamilton*, 647.

55 Ibid., 158.

56 Ibid., 708.

57 "Hail Hamilton at Dedication of Monument," *Chicago Daily Tribune*, July 7, 1952.

58 Orville Dwyer, "Grant Park Site for Hamilton Statue Refused," *Chicago Daily Tribune*, May 8, 1947.

JOHANN WOLFGANG VON GOETHE

59 Goethe, *Selected Verse*, 197.

60 Brandes, *Wolfgang Goethe*, 194.

61 Goethe, *Faust: Part I*, 43, 44; Goethe, *Faust: Part II*, Act 5, Sc. 23, lines 11936, 11937.

62 Goethe, *Maxims and Reflections*, 45, 117.

63 Goethe, *Selected Verse*, 280.

64 Special to the New York Times, "All Europe Our Mother," *New York Times*, June 15, 1914.

PHILIP SHERIDAN

65 Morris, Roy, Jr., *Sheridan*, 179.

66 Ibid., 213.

67 Ibid., 256.

68 Ibid., 375–376.

69 "Says it is Trivial," *Chicago Daily Tribune*, July 24, 1892.

AMERICAN INDIANS

70 "An Indian Memorial," *Chicago Daily Tribune*, May 6, 1884.

71 Rell, *Cyrus E. Dallin*, 39.

72 "Gives a Statue to Lincoln Park," *Chicago Daily Tribune*, January 22, 1894.

73 "His Signal of Peace," *Chicago Daily Tribune*, June 10, 1894.

JOHN PETER ALTGELD

74 Banard, *Eagle Forgotten*, 24.

75 Ibid., 228.

76 Ibid., 86–87.

77 Ibid., 405.

ENDNOTES

78 "Altgeld Contract Secretly Let to Gotham Sculptor," *Chicago Daily Tribune*, May 4, 1914.
79 Ibid.
80 Ibid.
81 "Unveil Statue of J.P. Altgeld," *Chicago Daily Tribune*, September 7, 1915.

RICHARD J. OGLESBY
82 Plummer, *Lincoln's Rail-Splitter*, 88.
83 Ibid., 200.
84 Ibid., 163.
85 "Oglesby Statue Unveiled with Lowden Tribute," *Chicago Daily Tribune*, November 22, 1919.

EUGENE FIELD
86 Conrow, *Field Days*, 35.
87 "Honor Memory of Poet Field with Statue," *Chicago Daily Tribune*, October 10, 1922.

GREENE VARDIMAN BLACK
88 Ring, *Dentistry*, 276.
89 Ibid., 204.
90 Ibid., 203.

MISSING PORTRAIT STATUES
91 "Tribute to the Master," *Chicago Daily Tribune*, June 20, 1897.
92 "A Bronze Bust of Emanuel Swedenborg by Adolf Jonsson in Lincoln Park, Chicago, Illinois," copyright property of The Academy of the New Church, accessed October 21, 2010, http://www.newchurchhistory.org/articles/jonsson/jonsson.php.
93 Ibid.

Bibliography

SELECTED BIBLIOGRAPHY FOR BIOGRAPHICAL SUMMARIES

LINCOLN
Donald, David Herbert. *Lincoln.* New York: Simon & Schuster, 1995.

LA SALLE
Danckers, Ulrich and Jane Meredith. *Early Chicago.* River Forest, IL: Early Chicago, Inc., 2000.
Johnson, Donald. *La Salle: A Perilous Odyssey from Canada to the Gulf of Mexico.* New York:
    Cooper Square Press, 2002.

FRANKLIN
Isaacson, Walter. *Benjamin Franklin: An American Life.* New York: Simon & Schuster, 2004.

GRANT
Ballard, Michael B. *U.S. Grant: The Making of a General, 1861–1863.* Lanham, Maryland:
    Rowman & Littlefield, 2005.
Perret, Geoffrey. *Ulysses S. Grant: Soldier & President.* New York: Random House, Inc., 1997.

ANDERSEN
Andersen, Hans Christian. *The Annotated Hans Christian Andersen.* Edited with and
    Introduction and Notes by Maria Tatar. Translations by Maria Tatar and Julie K. Allen.
    New York: W.W. Norton & Company, 2008.
Andersen, Jens. *Hans Christian Andersen: A New Life.* Translated by Tina Nunnally. New
    York: Overlook Duckworth, Peter Mayer Publishers, Inc., 2005.

SCHILLER
Heiseler, Bernt von. *Schiller.* Philadelphia: DuFour Editions, 1963.
Schiller, Friedrich von. *The Robbers and Wallenstein.* Translated by F. J. Lamport. New York:
    Penguin Books, 1979.
Thomas, Calvin. *The Life and Works of Schiller.* New York: AMS Press, Inc., 1970.
Witte, William. *Schiller.* Oxford: Basil Blackwell & Mott, Limited, 1949.

SHAKESPEARE
Greenblatt, Stephen. *Will in the World.* New York: W. W. Norton & Company, 2005.

HAMILTON

Chernow, Ron. *Alexander Hamilton.* New York: The Penguin Press, 2004.

GOETHE

Brandes, George. *Wolfgang Goethe.* New York: Crown Publishers, 1936.

Goethe, Wolfgang. *Faust: Part One.* Translated by Philip Wayne. New York: Penguin Books, 1949.

Goethe, Wolfgang. *Faust: Part Two.* Translated by David Luke. New York: Oxford University Press, 1994.

Goethe, Wolfgang. *Maxims and Reflections.* Translated by Elisabeth Stopp. Edited by Peter Hutchinson. New York: Penguin Books, 1998.

Goethe, Wolfgang. *Selected Verse.* Edited by David Luke. New York: Penguin Books, 1986.

Williams, John R. *The Life of Goethe.* Malden, Massachusetts: Blackwell Publishers Inc., 1998.

SHERIDAN

Morris, Jr., Roy. *Sheridan: The Life and Wars of General Phil Sheridan.* New York: Vintage Books, 1993.

AMERICAN INDIANS

"American Indian Tribes of Illinois," copyright 2000 Illinois State Museum, last modified October 2, 2002, http://www.museum.state.il.us/muslink/nat_amer/post/index.html.

Swenson, John F.. "Chicago: Meaning of the Name and Location of Pre-1800 European Settlements." *Early Chicago.* River Forest, IL: Early Chicago, Inc., 2000.

Tanner, Helen Hornbeck. "Tribal Mixtures in Chicago Area Indian Villages." *Early Chicago.* River Forest, IL: Early Chicago, Inc., 2000.

ALTGELD

Banard, Harry. *Eagle Forgotten.* Secaucus, New Jersey: Lyle Stuart, Inc., 1973.

Pacyga, Dominic A. *Chicago: A Biography.* Chicago: The University of Chicago Press, 2009.

OGLESBY

Plummer, Mark A. *Lincoln's Rail-Splitter: Governor Richard J. Oglesby.* Chicago: The University of Illinois Press, 2001.

FIELD

Conrow, Robert. *Field Days: The Life, Times & Reputation of Eugene Field.* New York: Charles Scribner's Sons, 1974.

BLACK

Ring (D.D.S., M.L.S., F.A.C.D.), Malvin E. *Dentistry: An Illustrated History.* New York: Harry N. Abrams, Inc., Publishers, 1985.

SELECTED BIBLIOGRAPHY FOR
STATUE DESCRIPTIONS AND INTRODUCTION

The American Midwest: An Interpretive Encyclopedia. Bloomington, IN: Indiana University Press, 2007.

Bach, Ira J., and Mary Lackritz Gray. *Guide to Chicago's Public Sculpture.* Chicago: University of Chicago Press, 1983.

Chicago Park District. Commissioners Office Division. *Principal Monuments—Memorials—Fountains, Etc., in the Park District.* (corrected copy) June, 1941.

Chicago Park District. Daniel Breen, Research Editor. *Historical Register of Park Districts, vol. 1, PT. 1,* 1941.

Chicago Park District. Department of Public Information. *Monuments and Memorials,* 1973.

Chicago Park District. Division of Public Information Service. *Monuments and Memorials,* 1961.

Chicago Park District. Office of the Commissioners. *Principal Monuments—Memorials—Fountains, Etc., in the Park District.* March 29, 1944.

Chicago Park District. Robert E. Moore, Landscape Architect. *Monuments and Memorials in the Chicago Park Districts,* 1936.

Chicago Tribune Historical Archive.

The Encyclopedia of Chicago. Chicago: University of Chicago Press, 2004.

Miller, Donald L. *City of the Century.* New York: Simon & Schuster, 2003.

Rell, Francis G. *Cyrus E. Dallin: Let Justice Be Done.* Rell G. Francis: 1976.

Riedy, James L. *Chicago Sculpture.* Chicago: University of Illinois Press, 1981.

Taft, Lorado. *Modern Tendencies in Sculpture.* Freeport, New York: Books for Libraries Press, 1970.

"The E.M. Viquesney 'Spirit of the American Doughboy' Database," Earl D. Goldsmith, Viquesney Researcher, last accessed October 26, 2010, http://doughboysearcher.weebly.com/chicago-lincoln-park-illinois.html.

"Hidden Truths: The Chicago City Cemetery and Lincoln Park," Pamela Bannos copyright 2010, site sponsored by Northwestern University sources, http://hiddentruths.northwestern.edu/.